Routledge Revivals

Paul Tillich

First published in 1973, this is the first book on Paul Tillich in which a sustained attempt is made to sort out and evaluate the questions to which Tillich addresses himself in the crucial philosophical parts of his theological system. It is argued that despite the apparent simplicity in his interest in the 'question of being', Tillich in fact conceives of the ontological enterprise in a number of radically different ways in varied contexts. Much of Professor Macleod's work is devoted to the careful separation of these strands in his philosophical thought and to an exploration and assessment of the assumptions associated with them.

This book will be of interest to readers of Tillich and philosophers who specialise in ontology and linguistics.

Paul Tillich

An Essay on the Role of Ontology in his Philosophical Theology

Alistair M. Macleod

First published in 1973
by George Allen & Unwin Ltd

This edition first published in 2017 by Routledge
2 Park Square, Milton Park, Abingdon, Oxon, OX14 4RN
and by Routledge
711 Third Avenue, New York, NY 10017

Routledge is an imprint of the Taylor & Francis Group, an informa business

© 1973 George Allen & Unwin Ltd

The right of Alistair M. Macleod to be identified as the author of this work has been asserted by them in accordance with sections 77 and 78 of the Copyright, Designs and Patents Act 1988.

All rights reserved. No part of this book may be reprinted or reproduced or utilised in any form or by any electronic, mechanical, or other means, now known or hereafter invented, including photocopying and recording, or in any information storage or retrieval system, without permission in writing from the publishers.

Publisher's Note
The publisher has gone to great lengths to ensure the quality of this reprint but points out that some imperfections in the original copies may be apparent.

Disclaimer
The publisher has made every effort to trace copyright holders and welcomes correspondence from those they have been unable to contact.

A Library of Congress record exists under LC control number: 73175689

ISBN 13: 978-1-138-09100-9 (hbk)
ISBN 13: 978-1-315-10831-5 (ebk)
ISBN 13: 978-1-138-09102-3 (pbk)

*CONTEMPORARY
RELIGIOUS THINKERS SERIES*

PAUL TILLICH
An Essay on the Role of Ontology
in his Philosophical Theology

Alistair M. Macleod
*Associate Professor of Philosophy
Queen's University, Canada*

First published in 1973

This book is copyright under the Berne Convention. All rights are reserved. Apart from any fair dealing for the purpose of private study, research, criticism or review, as permitted under the Copyright Act, 1956, no part of this publication may be reproduced, stored in a retrieval system, or transmitted, in any form or by any means, electronic, electrical, chemical, mechanical, optical, photocopying, recording or otherwise, without the prior permission of the copyright owner. Enquiries should be addressed to the publishers.

© George Allen & Unwin Ltd 1973

ISBN 0 04 111005 6 hardback
     0 04 111006 4 paper

To My Father and Mother

Preface

Instead of attempting to provide a reasonably comprehensive account of Paul Tillich's thought, I have used the space at my disposal to discuss at length one issue in his philosophical theology: the nature of the role played by ontology in his system. To narrow the scope of the discussion in this way seems to me to be justified for two reasons. In the first place, the issue to be discussed is clearly central to the evaluation of his thought: for it is as a *philosophical* theologian that Tillich has a claim to a secure place in the history of theology, and it is uncontroversial that in his view what the philosopher contributes to theology is an ontological doctrine. In the second place, Tillich's ontology exercises so pervasive an influence on his thought that a careful account of the diverse theoretical and practical concerns in which it is rooted seems to me to be an essential precondition of any more ambitious survey of his views.

I am grateful to Professor H. D. Lewis both for his advice in connection with the preparation of this book and for not making comprehensiveness of coverage a condition of its inclusion in the present series. To Professor C. A. Campbell I am deeply indebted for the care with which he read an earlier version of my work on Tillich and for encouraging me to believe that it was worth publishing. Finally, I should like to acknowledge the invaluable contribution my wife has made to the appearance of this book, chiefly by helping me to persevere in my Tillich studies at a time when my growing interest in other problems made it difficult to do so.

A debt of a different kind, to the C. D. Howe Foundation, ought not to go unrecorded: the final version of the manuscript was prepared during my tenure of a C. D. Howe Memorial Fellowship.

Oxford
July 28, 1971

A. M. M.

Contents

Preface	7
Biographical Notes	11
Introduction	15
1. The Religious Quest	21
2. Philosophical Anthropology	42
3. Ontology and Theology	58
4. The Conditions of Experience	76
5. Ontology and the Verb 'To Be'	88
6. The Mystery of Being	100
7. The Clarification of Concepts: I	119
8. The Clarification of Concepts: II	131
Conclusions	150
Bibliography	156

Biographical Notes

Paul Tillich was born in Starzeddel in East Germany in 1886, the son of a Lutheran minister. The religious and social environment in which he grew up was highly conservative and authoritarian. Between 1898 and 1904 he attended humanistic 'gymnasia' at Königsberg and Berlin, receiving an education in the classics and philosophy. After studying theology at the Universities of Berlin, Tübingen and Halle, he obtained in 1911 a doctorate in Philosophy from the University of Breslau for a dissertation on Schelling's philosophy of religion. He was ordained in 1912 into the ministry of the Evangelical Lutheran Church. He volunteered in 1914 for service in the German army and served for four years as a chaplain.

At the end of the First World War he took up an academic post in Theology at the University of Berlin. His experience of the war years and of the collapse of German society in which they ended had sharpened his sense of the inadequacy of the religious, philosophical and social traditions of the world into which he had been born. Immersing himself in the turbulent cultural and political life of post-war Berlin, he began work on the elaboration of a 'theology of culture' and became one of the major theoreticians of the religious socialist movement.

During the three semesters he spent as Professor of Theology at Marburg (1924-5) he encountered 'the first radical effects of the neo-orthodox theology on theological students: cultural problems were excluded from theological thought; theologians like Schleiermacher, Harnack, Troeltsch, Otto, were contemptuously rejected; social and political ideas were banned from theological discussions.' [1] Convinced of the need for a systematic

---

[1] Paul Tillich, 'Autobiographical Reflections' (in *The Theology of Paul Tillich*, ed. Kegley and Bretall. New York: Macmillan, 1961).

Paul Tillich

interpretation of theological doctrines in the light of fundamental cultural concerns, he embarked in 1925 on the task which was to occupy him for much of the rest of his life—the construction of a philosophical theology in which theological statements would be presented as furnishing answers to perennial human questions.

After brief appointments at the Universities of Dresden and Leipzig Tillich became in 1929 Professor of Philosophy at the University of Frankfurt, at that time (in Tillich's words) 'the most modern and most liberal university in Germany'. Increasingly well-known as an outspoken critic of the Nazi movement, he was dismissed from his professorship when Hitler became Chancellor of Germany in 1933.

Forced to leave his homeland at the age of 47, he moved with his family to the United States. His long and happy association with Union Theological Seminary in New York, where he was Professor of Philosophical Theology until 1955, was followed by a period at Harvard as a University Professor. These years saw the completion of his three-volume *magnum opus*.[2] When he died in 1965 he had been for more than a decade the dominant theological figure on the American intellectual scene. Although there has been some decline in his influence since his death, his *Systematic Theology* is sure to secure for him a lasting place in the history of theology.

PRINCIPAL WORKS BY TILLICH IN ENGLISH

The Religious Situation (New York: Henry Holt and Company, Inc., 1932; New York: Meridian Books, 1956).

The Interpretation of History (New York and London: Charles Scribner's Sons, 1936).

The Protestant Era (Chicago: University Press, 1948).

The Shaking of the Foundations (New York: Charles Scribner's Sons, 1948).

Systematic Theology, Vol. 1 (Chicago: University Press, 1951; London: Nisbet, 1953).

---

[2] *Systematic Theology* (the first volume appeared in 1951, the second in 1957 and the third in 1963).

Biographical Notes

The Courage To Be (New Haven: Yale University Press, 1952).
Love, Power and Justice (New York and London: Oxford University Press, 1954).
Biblical Religion and the Search for Ultimate Reality (Chicago: University Press, 1955; London: Nisbet, 1956).
The New Being (New York: Charles Scribner's Sons, 1955; London: S. C. M. Press, 1956).
Systematic Theology, Vol. 2 (Chicago: University Press, 1957; London: Nisbet, 1957).
Dynamics of Faith (London: George Allen & Unwin, 1957).
Theology of Culture (New York and London: Oxford University Press, 1959).
Morality and Beyond (New York and Evanston: Harper & Row, 1963).
Systematic Theology, Vol. 3 (Chicago: University Press, 1963; London: Nisbet, 1963).

Introduction

Paul Tillich died in 1965. During the last ten years or so of his life he was widely regarded as the most distinguished of twentieth-century theologians. Unlike Karl Barth, probably the only other recent theologian to enjoy comparable esteem among professional theologians, he had a considerable reputation among intellectuals with no formal connection with the Christian church. This certainly owed something to his life-long preoccupation with the question whether religion has any continuing role to play in a predominantly secular society. By arguing that the separation of the sacred and the secular is impoverishing to both, Tillich was able to engage the interest both of those who feared that their religious commitment had lost its relevance and of those whose secularist outlook was tinged with doubt about its adequacy as a philosophy of life.

Tillich was born in Germany in 1886. On the completion of his philosophical and theological studies he entered the ministry of the Evangelical Lutheran Church. Although he served for a time as an assistant pastor in various parishes and as an army chaplain during the First World War, virtually all of his long professional life was spent as a university professor. During his years in Germany—which came to an abrupt end in 1933 when he was dismissed from his university post for outspoken criticism of the Nazis—he was successively Lecturer in Theology at Berlin, Professor of the Science of Religion at Dresden, Professor of Theology at Leipzig and Professor of Philosophy at the University of Frankfurt. Expelled from his native land at the age of 47, Tillich moved with his family to New York, where as Professor of Philosophical Theology he began a long association with Union Theological Seminary which was to last until his

Paul Tillich

retirement in 1955. He was then invited to become a University Professor at Harvard University, a distinction reserved for the most eminent of academic figures. In this capacity he had no departmental responsibilities and was entitled to lecture on subjects of his own choice. His lectures were well attended and enthusiastically received. When he gave his last course of lectures at Harvard in 1962, several hundred students crowded into the lecture hall. His last appointment was at the University of Chicago. It was there, in 1963, that he published the final volume of his *Systematic Theology*. He was still very active when he died of a heart attack two years later in his eightieth year.

It is for the work he did on the boundary between philosophy and theology, and in particular for the system of philosophical theology to which he devoted a large part of his life, that Tillich will be remembered. Although the first volume of *Systematic Theology* did not appear until 1951, he began work on it some twenty-five years earlier. The second volume was published in 1957 and the third (and final) volume in 1963. Tillich seems not to have been altogether happy about the last volume. He published it under pressure from his publishers and was contemplating revising it at the time of his death. Among the other works of his maturity which throw light on his special conception of the contribution philosophy can make to systematic theology, three of the most important are *The Courage To Be* (1952), *Love, Power and Justice* (1954) and *Biblical Religion and the Search for Ultimate Reality* (1955).

It is an ironical fact that Tillich should have been at work on his system at a time in the history of philosophy and theology when both were markedly hostile, though for very different reasons, to his project. A theological climate in which Karl Barth was for much of this period the brightest sun was unfavourable to the enterprise of cultivating philosophical plants in the hope that they would bear theological fruit. Against the Barthians, consequently, Tillich had to try to show that philosophy has an indispensable contribution to make to theology. But he had the misfortune to believe in the necessity to theology

Introduction

of a kind of philosophy which has been in disfavour: modern philosophers have on the whole been sceptical of the possibility of the sort of metaphysical (or ontological) enterprise on the success of which Tillich pinned his hopes.

Special importance attaches, consequently, to two questions: first, whether he succeeded in vindicating the ontological enterprise in the face of philosophical doubts about it; secondly, whether he succeeded in demonstrating the relevance of ontology to theology. Much of this book is concerned with the first of these questions. Although I do not address myself directly to the second question, this is because the sort of negative answer I return to the first rules out the possibility of anything but a negative answer to the second.

The ontological enterprise is always represented by Tillich as consisting in the endeavour to answer a single question, '*the* ontological question'. This question, however, is itself formulated in many—*prima facie* different—ways. Consider the following, for example:

'The question regarding the character of the general structures that make experience possible is always the same. It is *the* philosophical question.' [1]

'But ontology asks the simple and infinitely difficult question: what does it mean *to be*? What are the structures, common to everything that is, to everything that participates in being?' [2]

'Philosophy asks the ultimate question that can be asked, namely, the question as to what being, simply being, means ... What is the meaning of being? Why is there being and not not-being?' [3]

'... the search for the basic meaning of love, power and justice individually must be our first task ... Ontology is the way in which the root-meaning ... of the three concepts of our subject can be found.' [4]

[1] Tillich, *Systematic Theology* (Vol. I), p. 22.
[2] Tillich, *Love, Power and Justice*, p. 19.
[3] Tillich, *Protestant Era*, p. 86.
[4] *Love, Power and Justice*, p. 2.

Paul Tillich

It is part of my purpose in this book to examine these and various other formulations of the ontological question, together with the assumptions (acknowledged and unacknowledged) which underlie them. It will be argued that they articulate quite different conceptions of the philosopher's task. If I am right an incoherence at the very heart of Tillich's philosophical thought will have been exposed. The unclarity of which almost all his critics complain (and which is perhaps the only common factor in their criticisms) will have been shown to be an irremediable unclarity, grounded as it is (in part, at any rate) in his failure to distinguish several quite different conceptions of ontology. Light will also be cast on the fact that startlingly different interpretations of Tillich have been offered. For if Tillich conflates several different versions of the ontological question in his philosophical writings, there cannot be a single correct account of his ontological position; there can only be interpretations giving prominence to this or that strand in his thought. This must be my excuse for not attempting to provide the sort of exposition of Tillich's ontological doctrines which the reader would otherwise have a right to expect.

No attempt is made to trace the development of Tillich's thought about the ontological question. Consequently virtually all the passages cited are from books and articles written after 1950. I hope in this way to undercut the objection that the various conceptions of ontology I attribute to Tillich do not all characterise his mature thought but merely mark stages in the evolution of his view of the philosopher's task.

I also make no attempt to trace the major influences on Tillich's thought about ontology. These are, of course, numerous and often transparent. It is clear, for example, that the Aristotelian conception of 'first philosophy' as the study of 'being *qua* being' has exerted a major influence, especially on the formation of the view discussed in the fifth chapter. The influence of Heidegger is acknowledged by Tillich to have been the source of one of the leading ideas of his philosophical theology—the idea that a philosophical anthropology might throw light on the

Introduction

nature of, and the necessity for, man's religious quest and thus enable the apologetic theologian to articulate the revelation-grounded message of Christianity in a relevant way. The influence of Kant is most evident in his description of the philosopher's central task as the exploration of the conditions of the possibility of experience. His debt to the Augustinian tradition is apparent in his rejection of the sort of 'natural theology' favoured by Thomists. And so on. Traces of the influence of practically every significant European philosopher are discoverable in Tillich's writings. (The notable exceptions—significantly—are the eighteenth-century British empiricists and their twentieth-century counterparts in the analytic movement.) But although Tillich's manifold indebtedness to other philosophers no doubt sheds light on the fact that he formulates the ontological question in several different ways, it is no part of my purpose in this book to try to trace the heterogeneous elements in his thought about ontology back to these sources. After all, knowledge of the ancestry of philosophical doctrines is neither a necessary nor a sufficient condition of determining what they mean and whether they are true.

Chapter 1

THE RELIGIOUS QUEST

'The search for ultimate reality ... is the ontological question, the root question in every philosophy.' [1]

'We philosophise because we are finite and because we know that we are finite. We are a mixture of being and nonbeing, and we are aware of it ... It is our finitude in interdependence with the finitude of our world which drives us to search for ultimate reality. This search is a consequence of our encounter as finite beings with a finite world. Because we stand between being and nonbeing and long for a form of being that prevails against nonbeing in ourselves and in our world, we philosophise.' [2]

'Every human being philosophises, just as every human being moralises and acts politically, artistically, scientifically, religiously ... Man is by nature a philosopher, because he inescapably asks the question of being.' [3]

The book from which these excerpts are taken—*Biblical Religion and the Search for Ultimate Reality*—contains 'a slightly extended version' of lectures delivered in 1951, the year of publication of the first volume of Tillich's *Systematic Theology*. It was the primary purpose of the lectures to explain and justify the role of ontology in Tillich's theological system. Although attention is focussed throughout the book on the nature of the

---

[1] Tillich, *Biblical Religion and the Search for Ultimate Reality*, p. 13.
[2] *Ibid.*, pp. 13–14.
[3] *Ibid.*, pp. 8–9.

Paul Tillich

ontological question—although, that is, Tillich's remarks about philosophical problems and procedures are by no means peripheral to his primary purpose in the lectures—two different conceptions of the philosophical enterprise are to be found in the book. At times, the 'search for ultimate reality' is represented as the search for an answer to a question about 'ultimate reality', the 'question of being' as Tillich prefers, for the most part, to call it. At other times—as in the passages from which excerpts were taken above—it is thought of as a search undertaken by human beings (*all* human beings; human beings *as such*) in an endeavour to come to terms with that anxiety which consists in their awareness of their 'finitude'—their awareness of the fact that they are 'a mixture of being and nonbeing' and that they 'stand between being and nonbeing'. Construed in the first of these ways, the 'search for ultimate reality' is an *intellectual* enterprise in which only *some* human beings (those who are 'philosophers' or 'ontologists') engage; construed in the second way, the 'search for ultimate reality' is the religious quest, in which (according to Tillich) *all* human beings are inescapably involved.

Thoroughly implausible though it is to *identify* the philosophical enterprise with the religious quest, it is only by doing so that Tillich is able to advance such surprising claims as that 'every human being philosophises' and that 'man is by nature a philosopher, because he inescapably asks the question of being'. My primary task in this chapter will be to try to account for Tillich's intermittent acceptance of this plainly unacceptable view of the relation between ontology and religion. Thereafter I shall draw attention to two (quite different) formulations of the ontological question which, while presupposing the distinctness of the ontological question and the religious quest, nevertheless owe something to Tillich's insistence on the closeness of the relation between them.

How is Tillich's occasional identification of the ontological question with the religious quest to be accounted for? The answer, in general terms, is that Tillich often describes the religious quest in a way which facilitates its confusion with the ontological

The Religious Quest

question. In elucidation and support of this answer I shall try to explain both (a) why Tillich thinks it is illuminating to describe the religious quest as a quest for *being* (or, in the language of *Biblical Religion and the Search for Ultimate Reality* as a 'search for ultimate reality') and (b) why this description of the religious quest makes it easy for him at times to obliterate the distinction between this *quest* and the ontological *question*.

I ANXIETY, THE THREAT OF NONBEING AND THE QUEST FOR BEING

Tillich's view that all human beings engage in the religious quest is bound up with his belief that there are certain anxieties from which all human beings suffer. It is these anxieties which generate the religious quest and a man's religion can consequently be seen as his way of coping with anxiety.

In *The Courage To Be*[4] Tillich identifies three anxieties to which human beings as such are alleged to be subject: the anxiety of death, the anxiety of guilt, and the anxiety of meaninglessness. The anxiety of death is occasioned by man's awareness of the fact that he is mortal, of the fact that he is destined some day to die. The anxiety of guilt is generated by man's awareness of the gap between what he is and what he ought to be. The anxiety of meaninglessness springs from man's sense of the ultimate purposelessness of the various activities which make up his life.

> 'In all three forms anxiety is existential in the sense that it belongs to existence as such and not to an abnormal state of mind as in neurotic (and psychotic) anxiety.'[5]
>
> 'The three types of anxiety are interwoven in such a way that one of them gives the predominant color but all of them participate in the coloring of the state of anxiety. All of them and their underlying unity are existential, i.e. they are implied in the existence of man as man, his finitude and estrangement.'[6]

It is unfortunate that Tillich should in this passage ground the

---
[4] pp. 50–4.
[5] Tillich, *The Courage To Be*, p. 41.
[6] *Ibid.*, p. 54.

Paul Tillich

claim that there are certain anxieties from which human beings as such suffer in certain ontological doctrines—the doctrines that human beings are 'finite' and 'estranged'. For one thing, there is an important strand in Tillich's thought about ontology (to be investigated in the next chapter) according to which these doctrines are themselves the *product*, not the *ground*, of a certain sort of analysis of the experience of 'existential anxiety'. Moreover, the assumption that the universality of 'existential anxiety' is an implication of the doctrines of finitude and estrangement stands in the way of unprejudiced consideration of the question *whether* the three anxieties distinguished are indeed universally experienced; and it is not at all evident that this question should be answered in the affirmative. Yet an affirmative answer is crucial to Tillich's insistence on the universality of the religious quest.

Now in the case of none of the anxieties distinguished by Tillich would it be natural to say that the quest it generates is a quest *for being*. The anxiety of death might plausibly be regarded as generating either a quest for immortality or (given a more pessimistic appraisal of our 'post-mortem' prospects) a quest for resigned acceptance of the fact that death is our final destiny;[7] but neither of these quests can be described, without further ado, as a quest for being. Again, while the anxiety of guilt might not unreasonably be taken to be the source of a quest for forgiveness and the anxiety of meaninglessness the source of a quest for a sense of purpose in life, neither of these quests, it would seem, can be illuminatingly characterised as a 'search for ultimate reality'. Why, then, does Tillich suppose that the religious quest generated by the experience of 'existential anxiety' can be appositely described as a quest *for being*?

The bald answer to this question can be easily supplied. Tillich

---

[7] It is necessary to allow for both possibilities because while the quest which might be thought to arise most naturally out of experience of the anxiety of death is the quest for survival of death, there are indications in Tillich's writings not merely that the quest in this form is incoherent—as presupposing that there is some possibility that the 'soul' is immortal, when in fact, on Tillich's view, there is no such possibility—but also that a recognition of the impossibility of survival of death is itself a presupposition of the experience of the anxiety of death (cf. *The Courage To Be*, p. 42).

The Religious Quest

thinks he can maintain that it is a quest for being which is generated by the experience of anxiety because he is convinced that this universal human anxiety has its source in 'the threat of nonbeing'. For if it is 'nonbeing' which gives rise to anxiety, the quest generated by the experience of anxiety can be represented naturally enough as a quest for whatever has the power to deal with 'the threat of nonbeing'—and it is 'being' which, according to Tillich, has the 'power to resist nonbeing'.

But how can Tillich suppose that the various anxieties he distinguishes in *The Courage To Be* all have their source in 'the threat of nonbeing'? Part of the answer lies in the sort of distinction he tries to draw between 'anxiety' and 'fear'. But as we shall see this would show (at best) only why he thinks *one* of the anxieties distinguished—viz. the anxiety of death—consists in 'the existential awareness of nonbeing'. To throw light on the claim that the same general account can be given of the anxieties of guilt and meaninglessness as well, notice must be taken both of Tillich's ambiguous use of the word 'anxiety' and of his insistence that the word 'nonbeing' has several senses.

Tillich's main reason for distinguishing sharply between fear and anxiety is that he wants to be able to admit that fears come and go—and that specific fears can be eliminated (at least in principle) by appropriate action—without being forced to abandon his conviction that anxiety forms the permanent and inescapable background to human life. Since he holds that fears are produced by and directed towards specific 'objects', the attempt to differentiate anxiety from fear takes the dramatic form of the claim that anxiety is occasioned by 'the negation of every object'—and 'the negation of every object' is, according to Tillich, 'nonbeing'.

> 'Fear, as opposed to anxiety, has a definite object (as most authors agree), which can be faced, analysed, attacked, endured ... But this is not so with anxiety because anxiety has no object, or rather, in a paradoxical phrase, its object is the negation of every object ... The only object is the threat

itself, but not the source of the threat, because the source of the threat is "nothingness".' [8]

'Anxiety is independent of any special object which might produce it; it is dependent only on the threat of nonbeing ... In this sense it has been said rightly that the object of anxiety is "nothingness"—and nothingness is not an "object". Objects are feared. A danger, a pain, an enemy, may be feared, but fear can be conquered by action. Anxiety cannot....' [9]

If Tillich were unprepared to endow nonbeing with any sort of ontological status, then the claim that nonbeing is the source of the threat which occasions anxiety would be either metaphorical or nonsensical. Tillich is emphatic, however, that 'nonbeing' is an indispensable ontological concept. Not only does he seriously entertain the question 'What sort of being must we attribute to nonbeing?' [10] but he commits himself to substantive assertions about man and the world which presuppose that in his view 'nonbeing'—despite the suggestions of the word—stands for *something*. Consider the following claims, for example: 'man participates not only in being but also in nonbeing'; [11] 'we are a mixture of being and nonbeing'; [12] 'there can be no world unless there is a dialectical participation of nonbeing in being'; [13] and 'being has nonbeing "within" itself as that which is eternally present and eternally overcome in the process of the divine life.' [14]

It is perhaps not altogether implausible to represent the anxiety occasioned by the awareness that some day one must die as a dread of ceasing to exist or of 'dissolving into nothingness'. Consequently if the horror of extinction were the distinctive element in what Tillich calls 'the anxiety of death', there would

[8] *The Courage To Be*, pp. 36–7.
[9] Tillich, *Systematic Theology* (Vol. I), p. 212.
[10] In one passage in *Systematic Theology* (pp. 207–8) he defends the legitimacy and importance of this question against both 'logical' and 'ontological' ways of 'trying to avoid' it (cf. *The Courage To Be*, p. 34).
[11] *Systematic Theology* (Vol. I), p. 208.
[12] *Biblical Religion and the Search for Ultimate Reality*, p. 11.
[13] *Systematic Theology* (Vol. I), p. 208.
[14] *The Courage To Be*, p. 34.

The Religious Quest

be some excuse for the view that *this* anxiety consists in 'the existential awareness of nonbeing'.[15] However, it is not simply the anxiety of death but anxiety *as such* which is said to have its source in 'the threat of nonbeing'. Now this larger claim—which lacks even the initial plausibility of the more limited claim about the source of the anxiety of *death*—is made the easier to advance by an ambiguity in Tillich's use of the term 'anxiety'. Sometimes 'anxiety' is used restrictively to refer to the anxiety of death; at other times it is used in a sense broad enough to cover the anxieties of guilt and meaninglessness as well. There is an unadvertised switch from the use of 'anxiety' in the restricted to its use in the more inclusive sense in the chapter of *The Courage To Be* [16] in which Tillich presents his 'ontology of anxiety'. Early in the chapter,[17] while attempting to establish a connection between anxiety and man's 'awareness of nonbeing', he uses 'anxiety' in the restricted sense. (The anxiety which is said to consist in 'the existential awareness of nonbeing' is simply the anxiety of death, as is clear from the fact that in elucidating this claim Tillich argues that 'it is not the realisation of universal transitoriness, nor even the experience of the death of others, but the impression of these events on the always latent awareness of our own having to die that produces anxiety'.) A few pages later,[18] however, it is by using 'anxiety' in the more inclusive sense that he is able to suggest that three types of anxiety should be distinguished. By overlooking the difference between this use and the narrower use presupposed by the claim that 'anxiety is the existential awareness of nonbeing', Tillich is able to take it as established that anxiety (in the more inclusive sense) is occasioned by 'the threat of nonbeing' and to propose that three types of anxiety (again in the inclusive sense of course) be distinguished 'according to the three directions in which nonbeing threatens being'.

[15] *Ibid.*, p. 35.
[16] Chapter 2, 'Being, nonbeing, and anxiety'.
[17] *The Courage To Be*, p. 35.
[18] *Ibid.*, p. 41.

Paul Tillich

'Nonbeing threatens man's ontic self-affirmation relatively in terms of fate, absolutely in terms of death. It threatens man's moral self-affirmation, relatively in terms of guilt, absolutely in terms of condemnation. It threatens man's spiritual self-affirmation relatively in terms of emptiness, absolutely in terms of meaninglessness.'

Thus, the claim that existential anxiety *as such* (and not the anxiety of *death* merely) is occasioned by 'the threat of nonbeing' is made the easier to advance by Tillich's failure to demarcate more carefully the scope of the statement that 'anxiety is the existential awareness of nonbeing', and his failure to do this is attributable in part to his ambiguous use of the term 'anxiety'.

It is also attributable in part to his ambiguous use of the term 'nonbeing'. While a common factor in most of Tillich's accounts of anxiety is his insistence that anxiety is a natural expression of the fact that human beings are 'a mixture of being and nonbeing', his use of the term 'nonbeing' in this context is far from univocal. For example, in the first volume of *Systematic Theology* Tillich explains that to say that 'everything which participates in the power of being is "mixed" with nonbeing' is equivalent to saying of it that 'it is finite'.[19] There then follow two quite different accounts of what this means. (a) On the one hand, Tillich identifies the 'finitude' of finite things with the fact that their existence is not an eternal existence—with the fact, that is, that they come into being and pass away. On this view, the 'nonbeing' which is said to be 'mixed' with their being 'appears as the "not yet" of being and as the "no more" of being'. To say of something that it is finite is to say that 'it is being in process of coming from and going towards nonbeing'. (b) But Tillich also claims that to be 'finite' is 'to be something', where 'to be something *is not* to be something else'. It is constitutive of the 'finitude' of finite things (in the sense now being given to 'finitude') that 'finite' beings *are not* (i.e. are not identical with) other finite beings: the 'nonbeing' with which 'being' is said to

---

[19] *Systematic Theology* (Vol. I), p. 211.

be 'mixed' in finite beings is their *not being* (identical with) other finite beings. Thus, to say of something that it is 'mixed' with 'nonbeing'—where this is held to be equivalent to saying of it that it is 'finite'—may involve saying either (a) that it is destined some day *not to be* (that is, not to exist) or (b) that it *is not* (identical with) other finite beings.

Elsewhere, however, Tillich is prepared to elucidate what is meant by the assertion that man is a 'mixture of being and nonbeing' in yet another way, this time by relating it to his contention that 'estrangement' is a fundamental feature of human existence.

> 'Even in what he considers his best deed nonbeing is present and prevents it from being perfect. A profound ambiguity between good and evil permeates everything he does, because it permeates his personal being as such. Nonbeing is mixed with being in his moral self-affirmation as it is in his spiritual and ontic self-affirmation. The awareness of this ambiguity is the feeling of guilt.' [20]

Here the 'nonbeing' which is an 'ingredient' of man's being consists not in his being destined some day *not to be*, nor in his *not being* (identical with) other finite beings, but in his *not being* what he 'potentially' or 'essentially' is—that is, in his *not being* what he ought to be.

Nor is it by inadvertence that the term 'nonbeing' is used in these different ways. When (in *The Courage To Be*) Tillich is elucidating the general doctrine that it is 'the threat of nonbeing' which generates 'existential anxiety', he relates the anxiety of death to the threat of 'ontic nonbeing', the anxiety of guilt to the threat of 'moral nonbeing', and the anxiety of meaninglessness to the threat of 'spiritual nonbeing'.[21] By insisting in this way on the many meanings of the term 'nonbeing', Tillich puts within his reach an answer of a sort to the charge that he has secured

---

[20] *The Courage To Be*, p. 52.
[21] *Ibid.*, p. 41 (cf. pp. 61–2). The index has an entry which reads 'Nonbeing: ... ontic, moral, spiritual. ...' (p. 195).

Paul Tillich

acceptance of his doctrine that 'existential anxiety' is occasioned by 'the threat of nonbeing' *merely* by exploiting the ambiguity in his use of the term 'anxiety'—that is, by providing a definition of 'anxiety' which fits (so far as it fits at all) the anxiety of death and then passing this off as a definition of anxiety as such, and as adequate, in consequence, to the anxieties of guilt and meaninglessness as well. For given his willingness to try to discriminate what he calls 'the qualities of nonbeing',[22] it is open to him to justify this broadening of the scope of a definition initially given with specific reference to the anxiety of death by claiming (as he does) that the 'nonbeing' which threatens 'man's ontic self-affirmation' (thereby generating the anxiety of death) is but one of several forms that 'nonbeing' may assume, and that two of the other forms it may assume pose a threat to man's *moral* and *spiritual* self-affirmation (thereby generating the anxieties of guilt and meaninglessness respectively). It may also be the case that his ambiguous use of the term 'nonbeing' contributes to his readiness to represent the three types of anxiety distinguished in *The Courage To Be* as necessarily connected phases or aspects of single anxiety: all three alike, after all, are said to be occasioned by 'the threat of nonbeing'. And of course the claim that there is a sense in which there is but *one* anxiety from which human beings suffer—despite the suggestion to the contrary implicit in the distinctions drawn between different types of anxiety—consorts well with the view that it is a *single* quest, the quest for being, which is generated by the experience of anxiety.

Now if Tillich affirms both (1) that human beings as such suffer from anxiety, and (2) that this anxiety, when differentiated from the psychological states (in particular, fears) with which it is liable to be confused, can be seen to have its source in 'the threat of nonbeing', then it is but a small step to the view that the fundamental human quest generated by the universal experience of anxiety is a quest *for being*. A small step perhaps, but a step nonetheless. Tillich feels entitled to take it, however, because in his view the 'being' sought by human beings in the grip

[22] *Ibid.*, p. 40.

The Religious Quest

of anxiety is characterisable—so far as it is characterisable at all —as that which has the 'power to conquer nonbeing'. 'What can we say fundamentally about the nature of being?' asks Tillich in *Love, Power and Justice*; and he replies:

> 'Nothing in terms of definition, but something in terms of metaphorical indication ... Being is power of being: power, however, presupposes, even in the metaphorical use of the word, something over which it proves its power ... What can that be which tries to negate being and is negated by it? There is only one answer possible: that which is conquered by the power of being is nonbeing.' [23]

In the light of this view of the relation between 'being' and 'nonbeing', it is easy to see how Tillich can at times represent the quest occasioned by experience of 'the threat of nonbeing' as a quest *for being*: for how could human beings in the grip of anxiety reasonably hope to come to terms with this threat if it were not by engaging in a quest for that which (allegedly) has the 'power to conquer nonbeing'—the power, that is, to overcome that which is the source of the threat which occasions anxiety?

II THE QUEST FOR BEING AND THE ONTOLOGICAL QUESTION

Having shown that there are elements in Tillich's thought which facilitate his acceptance of the view that human beings as such engage in a 'quest for being' or a 'search for ultimate reality', I turn now to consider the suggestion that Tillich occasionally confuses this view with the view that human beings as such ask the ontological question. That Tillich does make this latter claim is clear from such pronouncements of his as that 'every human being philosophises', that 'man is that being who asks the question of being', and that 'man is by nature a philosopher, because he inescapably asks the question of being'.[24] The oddity

---
[23] Tillich, *Love, Power and Justice*, p. 37.
[24] *Biblical Religion and the Search for Ultimate Reality*, pp. 8–9.

Paul Tillich

of his advancing so preposterous a claim will be diminished somewhat if it can be shown that it is advanced precisely because he sometimes confuses it with the claim (which he really does wish to make) that human beings as such engage in a quest for being. To this end I propose to examine, rather minutely, part of the passage in the second chapter of *Biblical Religion and the Search for Ultimate Reality* entitled 'Man and the Question of Being'.[25]

1. Tillich prepares the ground for the claim that 'man is that being who asks the question of being' by advancing and then analysing the view that 'man is the being who is able to ask questions'. Since this view—on *some* interpretation or other—is hardly likely to be contested, it is Tillich's interpretation of it which is of interest. This interpretation is presented in the form of an answer to a question about 'what it means to ask a question'. Asking a question, Tillich claims, 'implies, first that we do not have that for which we ask. If we had it, we would not ask for it'. But, equally, he continues, 'in order to be able to ask for something, we must have it partially; otherwise it could not be the object of a question'. Tillich's conclusion is that 'he who asks has and has not at the same time'.

Now it might be objected that, despite his professed intention of offering some account of what is involved in asking a question —where to ask a question is to ask a question *about* something, and to ask a question *about* something is to ask *about* it—Tillich in fact concentrates in this passage on what is involved in asking *for* something—where to ask for something is (at least very often) to make a request or demand. It is not a condition of this objection being put forward that there be any hard and fast line to be drawn between asking *for* something and asking *about* it. It is sufficient that there should be some standard uses of the 'asking for' idiom which have nothing to do with the asking of questions. And there are such uses. For example, if a man says to his wife, 'Give me the car-keys, please', he is certainly asking *for* the keys—but no *question* is being asked. If she replies: 'You had them last; where did you leave them?', she is (among other

[25] *Ibid.*, pp. 11–12.

The Religious Quest

things) asking a *question about* the keys—but she is not asking *for* them.[26]

Now so far as the *language* used in this passage is concerned, this objection seems to have some force. For not only is the 'asking for' idiom used throughout, but Tillich's use of it in close conjunction with the verb 'to have' strongly suggests that the 'asking for' under discussion has nothing to do with the asking of questions. In one of its commonest uses, my asking *for* something does indeed imply that I do not 'have' it: to ask *for* it is precisely to ask that it be *given* to me. My asking for the car-keys, for example, presupposes that I do not already 'have' them: the request is otiose if I am already securely (and knowingly) in possession of them. But of course in the sense of 'asking for something' in which it implies that the 'asker' does not already 'have' that *for* which he is asking, asking for something is normally not the same thing as asking a question.

There are two ways of mitigating the force of this objection. The first is to blunt the distinction between *asking for* and *asking about*. If there are uses of the 'asking for' idiom which are perfectly consonant with Tillich's declared intention of investigating what is involved in asking a question, then his use of the preposition 'for' after 'ask' on three of the four occasions of its occurrence in this passage [27] can be made the ground not even of a complaint that his language is misleading, and still less of a complaint

---

[26] This ambiguity in the use of 'asking for' is amusingly exploited in one of the Oz stories:

' "To learn is simple. Don't you ask questions?" inquired the Scarecrow.

"Yes; I ask as many questions as I dare; but some people refuse to answer questions."

"That is not kind of them," declared the Tin Woodman. "If one does not ask for information he seldom receives it; so I, for my part, make it a rule to answer any civil question that is asked of me."

"I am glad to hear this," said the Wanderer, "for it makes me bold to ask for something to eat." ' (*The Tin Woodman of Oz*, by L. Frank Baum (Chicago, Reilly & Lee, 1918), pp. 6–7).

[27] The fourth occasion of its use does not tell against the hypothesis that it is asking *for*, as distinct from asking *about*, that Tillich is actually discussing: in the sentence 'he who asks has and has not at the same time', there is certainly no explicit employment of the 'asking about' idiom, and the whole context strongly suggests that it is merely a terse formulation of some such sentence as 'he who asks for something has and has not that for which he asks'.

Paul Tillich

that he is not discussing what he professes to be discussing. The second way to try to mitigate the force of this objection is to consider Tillich's use of the 'asking for' idiom (and especially his use of this idiom in close conjunction with the verb 'to have') in the light of the substance of the argument he is developing, with a view to showing that the claims made are sheerly absurd if it is assumed, on the basis of the *language* he uses merely, that he is investigating what is involved in 'asking for' as *distinct* from 'asking about'. To try to defend Tillich in this way is to concede that his language may well be misleading without conceding that he has in fact abandoned his professed topic for another.

Now it must be granted that too much cannot be made to hang on Tillich's use of the preposition 'for' after the verb 'to ask'. There *are* uses of the 'asking for' idiom which are very closely related to—and might even be regarded as mere variants of—standard uses of the 'asking about' idiom. Is it not true, for example, that the asker of a question is, in asking, asking *for* something—an answer to his question, or information, for instance? If I ask someone at the weather office: 'What is the forecast for the week-end?' it is surely just as correct for me to describe what I am doing by saying that I am asking *for* weather information as it would be for me to say that I am asking *about* the weather. Now if there are such uses of the 'asking for' idiom, it cannot be inferred from the mere fact that Tillich uses this idiom that he has abandoned his professed topic for another. But it should be noted that on the occasions on which to ask a question *about* something is also to ask *for* something, *what* is asked *for* is not identical with what is asked *about*. Thus, to ask a question about the weather is indeed to ask *for*, let us say, *information* about the weather—but this is not the same as to ask for *the weather*! Now the trouble with Tillich's use of the 'asking for' idiom in this passage is that he does appear to assume that that *for* which we ask, when we ask a question, is *identical* with what the question is *about* (identical with what he calls 'the object of the question'). 'In order to ask for something, we must have it partially; otherwise *it* (i.e. that for what we ask) could not be the object of a question'. Thus, unless it can be shown that Tillich means something other than 'that about which a question is asked' by 'the object of a question', his use of the verb 'to ask for' in the passage under consideration does not coincide with that use of the 'asking for' idiom which would have enabled him to use the verb 'to ask for' with perfect propriety in the context of a discussion of what is involved in the asking of questions.

But although Tillich's language is misleading, as suggesting that he has in fact embarked on an examination of what is involved in the making of requests [28] despite his announced intention of investigating 'what it means to ask a question', the substance of the argument advanced in this passage suggests that it is question-asking, and not the making of requests, that Tillich is endeavouring to analyse. Can any sense be made of the claim that 'in order to be able to ask for something, we must have it partially' on the assumption that Tillich is here scrutinising the sort of 'asking for' which has no necessary connection with the asking of questions? What meaning could be given, for example, to the claim that in order to be able to 'ask for' the keys of the car, the asker must already 'have' them 'partially'? Now the fact that what Tillich says is unintelligible on the hypothesis that it is 'asking for' as *distinct* from 'asking about' that he is investigating is a reason for rejecting this hypothesis only if there is available an alternative hypothesis which permits more sense to be made of his claim in this passage. Is the claim, then, any more intelligible if we assume that Tillich—despite the suggestions of the language used—is in fact trying to make explicit a necessary condition of the asking of questions? I think it is. For if this assumption is made, it becomes possible to offer the following paraphrase of Tillich's argument in this passage: Asking a

---

[28] Strictly, the making of requests *of a certain sort*: for while all cases of asking for something are cases of making a request (or demand), not all cases of making a request are cases of asking for something. If I say 'Please phone the hospital', I am making a request all right, but what am I asking *for*?

Paul Tillich

question implies that we do not have the information for which we are asking ('if we had it, we would not ask for it'); but at the same time, in order to be in a position to ask for information about something, we must already have some information about it, otherwise it could not be the 'object' of our question. Now it must be admitted that even on this version of Tillich's argument, the claim that 'in order to be able to ask for something, we must have it partially' has a somewhat paradoxical ring. However, the paradoxical character of the claim that to ask for information is always to ask for *more* information can be mitigated by drawing a distinction between the sort of knowledge about something which is a precondition of asking a question about it and the sort of knowledge about it *lack* of which is a precondition of asking a question about it. Thus, while it may well be the case that there is a difference between the sort of knowledge I have if I merely know that A and B are names of places (and not of, say, events) and the sort of knowledge I have if I know what the distance is between A and B, it seems not unreasonable to maintain that in order to be in a position to ask how far it is from A to B, it must be the case both (a) that I know that A and B are places, and (b) that I am ignorant of the actual distance between them. Tillich's argument in this passage, then, cannot be dismissed as unintelligible if it is assumed that, despite the suggestions of the language he uses, he is endeavouring to give an account of what is involved in the asking of questions. Since parts at any rate of the argument must be so dismissed on the hypothesis that he actually undertakes an analysis of what is involved in the making of requests, it seems reasonable to acquit Tillich of the charge of having failed to do what he set out to do, though not of the charge that his language is misleading.

2. In the passage which follows, Tillich tries to make use of the general conclusion he has reached about what is involved in the asking of questions to throw light on his thesis that 'man is that being who asks the ontological question'. I want now to show that, in applying to the special case of the asking of the ontological question what he has concluded about the asking of

The Religious Quest

questions in general, Tillich is himself misled by the misleading language employed in his account of what it means to ask a question: consequently, although Tillich can be defended against the charge of confusing asking *about* with asking *for* in his general discussion, he does seem to be guilty of confusing 'asking about being' with 'asking for being'.

Consider what Tillich says.

> 'If man is that being who asks the question of being, he has and has not the being for which he asks ... We are a mixture of being and nonbeing. This is precisely what is meant when we say that we are finite. It is man in his finitude who asks the question of being.' [29]

Clearly, Tillich is trying to apply to the special case of the asking of the *ontological* question his general conclusion about what is involved in the asking of questions. His argument seems to proceed like this: *since* 'he who asks has and has not at the same time' (this being the general conclusion of his inquiry into what it means to ask a question), it must be true of the man who asks the question of being that 'he has and has not the being for which he asks'. Yet this, it will be clear, involves identifying asking the ontological question ('the question of being') with *asking for being*. Now if, as has been argued above, the meaning of 'he has and has not at the same time' in the general conclusion is, roughly, 'he both has and he has not *knowledge* about the object of his question', then Tillich has no right, in applying this general thesis to the special case of the ontological question, to claim that the man who asks the ontological question 'has and has not the *being* for which he asks'. What he *would* be entitled to claim is merely that the man who asks the ontological question 'has and has not *knowledge about* the "being" about which he asks'. But of course, had Tillich advanced *this* claim he would have been unable to ground the asking of the ontological question in man's 'finitude', for the context makes it plain that man's finitude is held by Tillich to consist, not in his limited *knowledge*, but in

[29] *Biblical Religion and the Search for Ultimate Reality*, p. 11.

Paul Tillich

his limited 'power of being'—that is, in his limited capacity to resist the threat of nonbeing. Thus, in advancing the claim that the man who asks the question of being 'has and has not the *being* for which he asks', Tillich is confounding asking *about* being (which is what he is supposed to be discussing) with asking *for* being. Tillich's view of man as 'finite' (as 'a mixture of being and nonbeing', as facing 'the threat of nonbeing') makes it intelligible that he should hold that man *qua finite* asks *for* being —where the 'being' sought is *that which has the power to resist nonbeing*. Yet the conclusion *in fact* drawn is that it is man's finitude which accounts for his *asking the ontological question*. It is because he fails to distinguish between asking *about* being and asking *for* being that Tillich is able to claim that 'we philosophise' because 'we stand between being and nonbeing and long for a form of being which prevails against nonbeing in ourselves and in our world'.[30] That is, the confusion of asking *about* being with asking *for* being—taken in conjunction with the contention that man is constrained by awareness of his 'finitude' to ask *for* being—must be held to be responsible for Tillich's preparedness to advance such startling claims as that 'every human being is by nature a philosopher, because he inescapably asks the question of being'.[31]

That it is not fanciful to accuse Tillich of confusing the ontological question with the quest for being generated by man's awareness of his finitude (i.e. by the experience of anxiety) is borne out by the passage which follows. In it Tillich tries to reinforce the claim that there is an intimate connection between the asking of the ontological question and man's experience of finitude by denying that the ontological question is one that is asked by *God*. Now, that God does not ask the ontological question might have been urged on the ground that He is omniscient and consequently does not need to ask it. Tillich's reason for insisting that God does not ask the ontological question is, however, quite different: it is that God is *omnipotent*.

[30] *Ibid.*, p. 14.
[31] *Ibid.*, p. 9.

The Religious Quest

'He who is infinite does not ask the question of being, *for, as infinite, he has the complete power of being.*' [32] This argument is intelligible, I suggest, only on the assumption that Tillich is tacitly identifying the question of being with the quest for being: for while it is indeed impossible to conceive of God asking *for* something he already possesses (viz. 'complete power of being'), it is by no means impossible to conceive of the asking of questions *about* what is 'fully possessed'. That God possesses the 'power of being' in full measure makes it unintelligible that he should engage in a quest *for* being, but it is hardly a reason for denying the intelligibility of his raising a question *about* that 'being' which he possesses in full measure.

III TWO WAYS OF CONNECTING THE ONTOLOGICAL QUESTION WITH THE RELIGIOUS QUEST

Although Tillich does in certain passages simply identify the religious quest with the ontological enterprise, he normally recognises that they are different while still insisting that there is a close *connection* between them. There are, I think, two main ways in which Tillich contrives to link the fact that human beings as such engage in the religious quest with the fact that some human beings (those, namely, who are philosophers) ask the ontological question.

1. On the one hand, the ontological question is represented as a question about what is sought by human beings in the religious quest. Since the religious quest is frequently characterised, for reasons which have been considered above, as a 'quest for being' or as a 'search for ultimate reality', the ontological question is represented as a question about the 'being' or 'ultimate reality' which is the object of the religious quest. This is the view of the ontological question which predominates in *Biblical Religion and the Search for Ultimate Reality*. This view involves the virtual obliteration of the distinction normally drawn by Tillich between the sort of question about being to which the ontologist can hope to return an answer and the sort

[32] *Ibid.*, pp. 11-12.

of question about God to which an answer can be returned only on the basis of revelation.[33]

2. The second main way in which Tillich contrives to connect the ontological question with the religious quest is by representing the ontological question as one concerning the features of the human situation which throw light on the fact that the religious quest is one in which human beings necessarily engage. On this view the ontologist is required to contribute the sort of doctrine of man which will render intelligible the fact that there is a certain quest—viz. the quest for being—which human beings as such undertake. There is a hint of such a view in the language employed by Tillich in the passage which was scrutinised in the last section: for in characterising man as 'that being who asks the question of being' (and in this context, as has been noted, Tillich must be taken to mean by 'that being who asks the question of being' 'that being who engages in the quest for being or the search for ultimate reality') Tillich says of man that he is 'finite', that his 'power of being is limited', and that he is a 'mixture of being and nonbeing'—all pronouncements which Tillich in other places regards himself as entitled to make *in his capacity as an ontologist*. This hint is not, however, followed up. Instead, as has been noted, the ontological question is represented in *Biblical Religion and the Search for Ultimate Reality* as a question about that 'utlimate reality' which is the object of the religious quest.

In the philosophical parts of *Systematic Theology*, however, the central doctrines enunciated by Tillich the ontologist—that human beings are 'finite' and 'estranged'—are designed to throw light on the religious quest by providing the sort of description of the human situation which will make it clear why the quest for being (or the search for ultimate reality) is a universal human quest. For it is in virtue of their 'finitude' and 'estrangement' that human beings experience the anxieties of death and guilt, and it is these anxieties, of course, which are the source of the religious quest. A similar view of the ontologist's task is adopted in *The*

[33] This view of the ontological question is discussed in Chapter 3.

The Religious Quest

Courage To Be. The differentiation of those 'existential' anxieties which give rise to the religious quest from the 'pathological' anxieties which are the objects of the healing art of the psychiatrist requires, according to Tillich, 'an ontological understanding of human nature'. The distinction between existential and pathological anxiety 'cannot be made by depth-psychological analysis alone; it is a matter of ontology'. 'Only in the light of an ontological understanding of human nature can the body of material provided by psychology and sociology be organised into a consistent and comprehensive theory of anxiety.'[34] Tillich notes that the 'lack of an ontological analysis of anxiety and of a sharp distinction between existential and pathological anxiety' has stood in the way of fruitful collaboration between 'ministers and theologians' on the one hand and 'physicians and psychotherapists' on the other. He consequently expresses the hope that 'some principles for the co-operation of the theological and medical faculties in dealing with anxiety' can be derived from 'ontological analysis'. The 'basic principle' which his ontological doctrine of man makes it possible for him to enunciate is 'that existential anxiety in its three main forms is not the concern of the physician *as* physician, although he must be fully aware of it; and, conversely, that neurotic anxiety in all its forms is not the concern of the minister *as* minister, although he must be fully aware of it'.[35] In short, the religious quest generated by the experience of 'existential anxiety' can be illuminated by the ontologist if he takes it to be his task to provide the sort of doctrine of man which will identify the features of the human predicament which give rise to 'existential anxiety'. The view of the philosopher's task which makes possible the forging of a link of this sort between the religious quest and the ontological question will be the topic of the next chapter.

[34] *The Courage To Be*, p. 65.
[35] *Ibid.*, pp. 72–3.

Chapter 2

PHILOSOPHICAL ANTHROPOLOGY

It is one of Tillich's deepest convictions as a theologian that philosophy has an indispensable role to play in 'systematic theology'. He rejects the view (stated most powerfully, among recent theologians, by Karl Barth) that it is possible for the theologian to provide an adequate systematic interpretation of the Christian message by focussing attention exclusively on those revelatory events which are held by Christians to be the source of this message. But in rejecting a 'theology of revelation' which turns its back on philosophy, he does not place himself squarely in the tradition of so-called 'natural theology'. He finds it necessary to deny what he takes to be the central affirmation of the philosophical theologians who belong to this tradition, which is that it is possible to make statements about God on purely philosophical grounds—that is, independently of revelation. I want to examine in this chapter Tillich's programme for a philosophical theology which would provide an alternative both to traditional theologies of revelation and to traditional natural theologies, with a view to drawing attention to a certain conception of the philosopher's task to which this programme commits him.

I PHILOSOPHICAL THEOLOGY AND THE METHOD OF CORRELATION

The method Tillich advocates and professes to adopt in his work as a 'systematic theologian' is the method of 'correlation'. The systematic theologian is charged, according to Tillich, with

Philosophical Anthropology

a double responsibility: first, he must be faithful to the content of the revelation it is his task to interpret; secondly, he must try to interpret it in a way which makes it intelligible even to those who do not share his religious commitment. The first of these requirements reflects Tillich's conviction that statements about God can be made only on the basis of revelation; the second underlines the apologetic character of the systematic theologian's task. The systematic theologian who employs the method of correlation can hope to satisfy both requirements by seeking to connect ('correlate') questions which are asked by human beings quite independently of revelation with statements which can be made only on the basis of revelation. For this connection to be established, of course, it will have to be the case both (a) that the questions are such that no answers to them can be derived from sources other than revelation, and (b) that the statements derivable from revelation can be represented as at least possible answers to these questions. (a) is important because without it there will be answers to these questions other than those which are grounded in relevation—and yet part of what makes it necessary, on Tillich's view, for a philosophical theology of the sort he has in mind to be constructed is the unavailability of any answer to these questions which is not grounded firmly in revelation. (b) is essential, of course, because without it the statements made by the theologian on the basis of revelation will seem irrelevant to those without any religious commitment. To establish a connection in this way between questions human beings are disposed to ask quite independently of revelation and statements (derivable only from relevation) which answer these questions is to *correlate* what Tillich calls 'existential questions' with 'theological answers'. A systematic theology which employs the method of 'correlation' (in this sense) will be able to satisfy simultaneously both the demand that the theologian be faithful to the content of the revelation it is his task to interpret and the demand that this interpretation assume a form which renders the message grounded in this revelation intelligible to those without any religious commitment.

Paul Tillich

Tillich's advocacy of the method of correlation sets him apart, in his own view, from theologians of three kinds: 'supranaturalists', 'naturalists' (or 'humanists'), and 'dualists'.

The 'supranaturalists' (of whom Barth is often singled out for mention by name) are accused by Tillich of not even trying to establish a 'point of contact' between the theological statements they make on the basis of revelation and the questions which human beings with no religious commitment are asking. It is their view (according to Tillich) that 'the "situation" cannot be entered; no answer to the questions implied in it can be given, at least not in terms which are felt to be an answer. The message must be thrown at those in the situation—thrown like a stone'.[1] They take the Christian message to be 'a sum of revealed truths which have fallen into the human situation like strange bodies from a strange world'.[2] Tillich's objection to this view is that it not only fails to render theological statements intelligible to those with no religious commitment but also leaves unanswered fundamental questions which human beings are asking and to the answering of which the Christian message is highly relevant. 'Man cannot receive answers to questions he never has asked. Furthermore, man has asked and is asking in his very existence and in every one of his spiritual creations questions which Christianity answers.'[3]

Of the method adopted by the 'naturalists' or 'humanists' Tillich says that 'it derives the Christian message from man's natural state. It develops its answer out of human existence, unaware that human existence itself *is* the question'. This was the method adopted by 'much of liberal theology in the last two centuries'. The 'contents of the Christian faith were explained as creations of man's religious self-realisation in the progressive process of religious history'.[4] Tillich's objection to this theological method is that it presupposes the possibility of deriving answers to 'existential questions' from scrutiny of the human

---
[1] Tillich, *Systematic Theology* (Vol. I), p. 7.
[2] *Ibid.*, p. 72.
[3] *Ibid.*, p. 73.
[4] *Ibid.*, p. 72.

Philosophical Anthropology

situation: the unavailability of such answers is, from Tillich's point of view, an essential part of the thesis (to which, as has been noted, he subscribes) that revelation has an indispensable role to play in the answering of 'existential questions'. Thus, while for the 'naturalist' (or 'humanist') 'questions and answers' are 'put on the same level of human creativity', everything being said '*by* man, nothing *to* man', for Tillich 'revelation is "spoken" to man, not by man to himself'.[5]

The third method rejected by Tillich is the 'dualistic' method employed by 'natural theologians' who, while rejecting (with Tillich) the 'naturalist' view that it is possible to derive from scrutiny of the human situation answers to 'existential questions', nevertheless 'posit a body of theological truth which man can reach through his own efforts'—that is, independently of revelation. Unlike the 'naturalist', the 'dualist' recognises 'the infinite gap between man's spirit and God's spirit' yet is not deterred by the existence of this gap from attempting to formulate a doctrine of God independently of revelation.[6] The 'so-called arguments for the existence of God' are, in Tillich's view, the most important part of the 'natural theology' which is the product of this attempt. Tillich's rejection of the 'dualist' method—and with it his rejection of 'natural theology'—is grounded in his belief that the 'gap between man's spirit and God's spirit' makes man completely dependent upon revelation for knowledge of God.

Tillich's rejection of natural theology does not, of course, imply hostility to philosophical theology as such. On the contrary, it is Tillich's view that the systematic theologian who uses the method of correlation is himself a philosophical theologian of a special sort. This is because he believes that philosophy has an indispensable contribution to make to systematic theology. Although it is supposed to be no part of the philosopher's job to make his contribution in the form of a doctrine of God, it is, according to Tillich, one of his tasks to ensure the adequate

[5] *Ibid.*, p. 73 (my italics).
[6] *Ibid.*, p. 73.

Paul Tillich

formulation of those 'existential questions' to which statements about God provide possible answers.

But what does this philosophical task amount to? There seem to be two rather different answers in Tillich's writings. On the one hand, it is maintained that it is by 'analysis of the materials made available by man's creative self-interpretation in all realms of culture'—in 'poetry, drama, the novel, therapeutic psychology, and sociology', for example—that the philosopher is able to formulate 'existential questions' adequately: on this view the 'situation' which the philosopher seeks to analyse and with which he must have the sort of familiarity which is a condition of such analysis is 'the totality of man's creative self-interpretation in a special period'.[7] On the other hand, it is maintained that it is in the light of an analysis of what is involved in being a human being that the philosopher is able to formulate these questions adequately: on this view, the 'situation' which the philosopher seeks to analyse is the 'human situation'—where this is a 'situation' with which we are necessarily familiar simply in virtue of the fact that we are human beings.[8]

II PHILOSOPHICAL ANTHROPOLOGY AND THE DOCTRINES OF FINITUDE AND ESTRANGEMENT

It is the second of these views of the philosopher's role in relation to the construction of a systematic theology which is predominant in Tillich's thought. An examination of the central doctrines presented in the philosophical parts of his system will serve to show that it is primarily in the light of a philosophical doctrine of man rather than in the light of a critical scrutiny of 'man's creative self-interpretation in every realm of culture' that Tillich works his way towards a formulation of those 'existential questions' to which statements about God derived from revelatory sources provide possible answers. I turn now to the examination of these doctrines.

[7] *Ibid.*, p. 71.
[8] *Ibid.*, p. 4.

Philosophical Anthropology

What these central doctrines are is clearly indicated by the following passage, which purports to describe summarily the structure imparted to Tillich's system by his employment of the method of correlation.

'The structure of the theological system follows from the method of correlation. The method of correlation requires that every part of the system should include one section in which the question is developed by an analysis of human existence and existence generally, and one section in which the theological answer is given ... This division must be maintained. It is the backbone of the structure of the present system ... In so far as man's existence has the character of self-contradiction or estrangement, a double consideration is demanded, one side dealing with man as he essentially is (and ought to be) and the other dealing with what he is in his self-estranged existence (and should not be) ... Therefore one part of the system must give an analysis of man's essential nature (in unity with the essential nature of everything that has being), and of the question implied in man's finitude and finitude generally; and it must give the answer which is God. This part, therefore, is called "Being and God". A second part of the system must give an analysis of man's existential self-estrangement (in unity with the self-destructive aspects of existence generally) and the question implied in this situation; and it must give the answer which is the Christ. This part, therefore, is called "Existence and the Christ".' [9]

This passage makes it clear that the central affirmations about human beings made in the 'question-developing' parts of Tillich's systematic theology are (a) that human beings are 'finite', and (b) that human beings are 'estranged'.

Now there is no evidence that a necessary condition of Tillich's being in a position to advance these theses is that he carry through an analysis of the various 'cultural forms' in which human beings express their interpretation of their existence. On

[9] *Ibid.*, p. 74.

the contrary, it seems to be sufficient that the philosopher attend critically to certain 'universally human' experiences—experiences, that is, which human beings have under all sorts of social and cultural conditions. As Tillich puts it in the introduction to the second volume of *Systematic Theology* (in a passage designed to remind readers of what the user of the method of correlation is committed to trying to do when he endeavours to formulate 'existential questions' adequately), the philosopher must

> 'participate in the human predicament not only actually—as he always does—but in conscious identification. He must participate in man's finitude, which is also his own, and in its anxiety as though he had never received the revelatory answer of "eternity". He must participate in man's estrangement, which is also his own, and show the anxiety of guilt as though he had never received the revelatory answer of "forgiveness".' [10]

In other words, in order to be in a position to formulate 'existential questions' effectively, it is sufficient that the philosopher scrutinise certain experiences with which he is necessarily familiar in virtue of the fact that he is a human being—in particular, the experience of 'the anxiety of death' and the experience of 'the anxiety of guilt'. The contention that human beings are 'finite' represents an attempt on Tillich's part to identify the feature of the human situation which gives rise to the universal experience of 'ontic anxiety' ('the anxiety of death'). The contention that human beings are 'estranged' represents his attempt to identify the feature of the human situation which gives rise to the universal experience of the 'anxiety of guilt'. Tillich's central doctrines of human finitude and estrangement are thus the products of a certain sort of analysis of experiences which human beings as such are alleged to have.

Nor is it surprising that Tillich should hold that doctrines suggested by scrutiny of these experiences facilitate the adequate formulation of 'existential questions', thereby throwing light on

[10] *Ibid.*, (Vol. II), pp. 16–17.

Philosophical Anthropology

the force of theological statements made on the basis of revelation. For Tillich holds that the very experience scrutiny of which yields the philosophical doctrine of human finitude is also the experience in virtue of which human beings 'can understand what the notion of God means'. 'Only those who have experienced the shock of transitoriness, the anxiety in which they are aware of their own finitude, the threat of nonbeing, can understand what the notion of God means.' [11] If the receptivity of human beings to revelation is a function of the fact that they are creatures subject to 'existential anxiety', then it is natural that the systematic theologian whose task it is to 'correlate' statements made on the basis of revelation with questions asked by human beings independently of revelation should seek to articulate these questions in the light of an analysis of man's experience of this anxiety.

Tillich is not averse, of course, to taking into consideration what is said about the human predicament by 'creative representatives of various realms of culture': by poets, novelists, psychologists and sociologists, for example. It is not on the *basis* of what they say, however, that Tillich presents his central doctrines about the human situation. Rather, what they say is regarded either as illustrating these doctrines or as subject to amendment in the light of these doctrines. Both points are illustrated by the use Tillich makes of the Freudian doctrine of libido. On the one hand, he commends Freud for noting that 'it is the never satisfied libido in man, whether repressed or unrestrained, which produces in him the desire to get rid of himself as man': in 'these observations concerning man's "discontent" with his creativity', Tillich maintains, Freud 'looks deeper into the human predicament than many of his followers and critics'. Yet on the other hand, Tillich is careful to add that 'theology cannot accept Freud's doctrine of libido as a sufficient reinterpretation of the concept of concupiscence'—'concupiscence' being one of the marks of human 'estrangement' and Tillich's account of concupiscence an important part, consequently, of his doctrine of 'estrangement'. 'Freud did not see that his description of human nature is adequate

[11] *Ibid.* (Vol. I), p. 69.

Paul Tillich

for man only in his existential predicament and not in his essential nature.'[12] Freud's 'doctrine of libido' is thus endorsed by Tillich so far as it coincides with an important part of his own doctrine of estrangement; and elements in the Freudian doctrine which are at variance with his doctrine are rejected. The insights into the human situation embodied in Tillich's central doctrines of finitude and estrangement are clearly regarded by him as achievable independently of scrutiny of what is said about the human situation by 'creative representatives in every realm of culture'.

The ultimate ground of Tillich's rejection of certain analyses of the 'human predicament' offered by 'creative representatives in various realms of culture' is disclosed in his attitude towards those 'psychological and sociological analyses' according to which 'the evil of man's predicament' can be derived from 'the structure of industrial society'. Tillich argues that if the human predicament exposed in these analyses were a mere consequence of certain features of life in an industrial society, then it would be reasonable to hope that 'changes in the structure of our society would, as such, change man's existential predicament'. It would, moreover, be pointless to try to make use of such analyses in the formulation of 'existential questions', for any questions on which these analyses could throw light would not be 'existential questions' at all—simply because they would not call for 'theological answers'. Against such analyses of the human situation Tillich maintains that 'estrangement is a quality of the structure of existence' and that 'man's estrangement from his essential being is the universal character of existence'.[13]

The claim that 'estrangement is a quality of the structure of existence'—which is the ground, as has been seen, of Tillich's denial that 'the evil of man's predicament' is derivable from 'the structure of industrial society'—is at first sight not the sort of claim one would expect the philosopher to be in a position to advance on the basis of the type of analysis of the human situation

[12] *Ibid.* (Vol. II), pp. 61–2.
[13] *Ibid.*, pp. 85–6.

Philosophical Anthropology

which it is apparently his main task to undertake. For even if the experience of the anxiety of guilt were (as Tillich claims) a universal human experience, and even if (as he also claims) this experience were analysable in terms of man's awareness of his 'estrangement', 'estrangement', it would seem, could at best be represented as a 'quality of the structure' of *human* existence, not of existence as such. It is, however, the larger claim that 'estrangement is a quality of the structure of *existence*' (and not merely of *human* existence) that Tillich considers it essential to maintain on the basis of his analysis of the human situation. Tillich maintains, that is, that his analyses of the human situation embody insights into the nature of being or existence as such, not simply insights into the nature of *human* existence. In the passage which was quoted at the beginning of this section for example, Tillich insists that the 'question-developing' sections of his system must contain 'an analysis of human existence *and existence generally*'; also that one of these sections must contain 'an analysis of man's essential nature (*in unity with the essential nature of everything that has being*) and of the question implied in man's finitude *and finitude generally*'; also that another of these sections must contain 'an analysis of man's existential self-estrangement (*in unity with the self-destructive aspects of existence generally*)'.[14] It is this feature of Tillich's conception of the philosopher's task in relation to systematic theology which makes it possible for him to deny that it is a 'doctrine of man' which is contributed by the philosopher to the system.

> 'Whoever has penetrated into the nature of his own finitude can find traces of finitude in everything that exists. And he can ask the question implied in his finitude as the question implied in finitude universally. In doing so, he does not formulate a doctrine of man; he expresses a doctrine of existence as experienced in him as man.' [15]

Tillich is not going back, of course, on his view that an analysis of the human situation is indispensable to the proper formulation

[14] *Ibid.* (Vol. I), p. 74 (my italics).
[15] *Ibid.*, p. 70.

Paul Tillich

of 'existential questions'. He is claiming, rather, that in getting clear about what it means to be a human being (that is, in analysing the human situation) the philosopher is simultaneously getting clear about what it means for anything which exists to exist. To ascertain the structure of *human* existence is *at the same time* to ascertain the structure of existence as such. Tillich's denial that it is a 'doctrine of man' which is the fruit of 'analysis of the human situation' is to be understood, consequently, in the context of the claim that such analysis can be expected to yield insight into the nature of being or existence as such: in short to yield an ontology. Why Tillich should have an interest in complicating in this way his account of the task of the philosopher whose analysis of the human situation is supposed to throw light on 'existential questions' I shall consider in the next section.

III PHILOSOPHICAL ANTHROPOLOGY AND ONTOLOGY

There are two problems faced by Tillich on which light is shed by his claim that the sort of analysis of the human situation to be found in the philosophical parts of his theological system embodies an account of existence or being as such, and not merely a doctrine of man. The first of these problems concerns the very possibility of ontology, the second the differentiation of religious from non-religious needs. A solution to both seems to be put within his reach by the claim that no sharp distinction can be drawn between a certain sort of philosophical anthropology and ontology.

1. Despite his claim that it is the ontologist's task to ascertain the characteristics possessed by all beings (the characteristics 'common to everything that is' [16]), and despite his explicit contention that 'there is no particular place to discover the structure of being' and that the ontologist must consequently look in 'all places' for an answer to his question,[17] Tillich is

[16] Tillich, *Love, Power and Justice*, p. 19.
[17] *Systematic Theology* (Vol. I), p. 27.

Philosophical Anthropology

sometimes beset by doubts about the very possibility of the ontological enterprise so conceived. The basic reason for these doubts is his belief that the beings in which the ontologist is interested cannot be identified with the objects of experience: what a thing is in itself is not identical, Tillich holds, with what it is *qua* object of someone's experience.

Three points are worth noting. First, it is a condition of this being given as a reason for doubting the possibility of ontology that it is the fundamental characteristics of beings *as they are in themselves*—as distinct from *qua* objects of human experience—which the ontologist must seek to ascertain. As will be noted in a later chapter,[18] there is a strand in Tillich's thought about the ontological question which involves abandonment of just this assumption: for in some passages it is the features common to the objects of experience which Tillich takes it to be the ontologist's task to discover. Second, Tillich rejects the view that the ontologist is in a position to penetrate to the innermost nature of beings as they are in themselves by the use of 'pure reason': he agrees with Kant that human beings have the power neither to apprehend intuitively the nature of 'things in themselves' nor to exercise their rational faculties discursively concerning what lies beyond the bounds of experience. In claiming for ontology a central place as a philosophical discipline Tillich is careful to deny that ontology is a 'speculative-fantastic attempt to establish a world behind the world'; indeed it is because he thinks that 'the preposition *meta* (in metaphysics) now has the irremediable connotation of pointing to a duplication of this world by a transcendent realm of beings' that he regards it as 'less misleading to speak of ontology instead of metaphysics'.[19] Finally, scepticism about the possibility of providing any answer to the ontological question would be a natural consequence of inability to specify some way of gaining cognitive access to the 'nature of being' which involves neither an unwarranted transcendence of experience nor any arrogant

[18] Chapter 4.
[19] *Systematic Theology* (Vol. I), p. 24.

pretension to the possession of rational powers which human beings lack.

Tillich is able to avoid scepticism about the possibility of ontology because he conceives of 'man as that being in whom all levels of being are united and approachable'.

> 'Man occupies a preeminent position in ontology, not as an outstanding object among other objects, but as that being who asks the ontological question and in whose self-awareness the ontological answer can be found.'
> 'Man is able to answer the ontological question himself because he experiences directly and immediately the structure of being and its elements.' [20]
> 'Whenever man has looked at his world he has found himself in it as a part of it. But he has also realised that he is a stranger in the world of objects, unable to penetrate it beyond a certain level of scientific analysis. And then he has become aware of the fact that he himself is the door to the deeper levels of reality, that in his own existence he has the only possible approach to existence itself. This does not mean that man is more approachable than other objects as material for scientific research. The opposite is the case! It does mean that the immediate experience of one's own existing reveals something of the nature of existence generally.' [21]

Thus, while human beings are prevented by their limited cognitive powers from ascertaining directly the fundamental features of beings other than themselves, they have the means of discovering in their own case what the fundamental features of their existence are—through attention to the 'immediate experience of existing'. And since man is 'that being in whom all levels of being are united', the features which are fundamental to human existence can be assumed to be fundamental to other beings as well.

Thus, Tillich's problem concerning the possibility of ontology is resolved by representing 'man as the entering door to ontology'.

[20] *Ibid.*, p. 187.
[21] *Ibid.*, p. 70.

Philosophical Anthropology

It is just this anthropological approach to the solution of the ontological problem which enables him to deny that it is a mere philosophical anthropology which is the outcome of 'analysis of the human situation': the results of such analysis, he can claim, are indicative of the structure not only of human existence but of existence as such.

2. Tillich's representation of the doctrine of man elaborated in the philosophical parts of his theological system as an *ontological* doctrine is also not unconnected with his desire to provide a secure foundation for the claim that human beings necessarily engage in a quest which is not capable in principle of being fulfilled by human effort. It has already been noted (in Chapter 1) that there are passages in his writings in which Tillich seems to confuse this quest with the ontological question. It has also been pointed out that one of the two main ways in which Tillich tries to establish a connection between this quest and the ontological question (while recognising, of course, that they are not identical) is by assigning to the philosopher the task of so describing the human situation as to lend support to the claim that human beings necessarily engage in such a quest. Now for this to be done, this quest must be represented as arising out of certain universal and ineradicable features of the human situation. It is not sufficient that the quest be traced to its source in features of the human situation which are contingent on the existence of certain social or cultural conditions: if it had such a source, it could not be expected to survive the disappearance of these conditions and it could not, consequently, be held to be a universal human quest. The reason for the requirement that this quest be represented as generated by features of the human situation which human beings are powerless to eliminate is that this quest is, on Tillich's view, the *religious* quest, and Tillich's whole theological system is constructed in the belief that the religious quest requires for its fulfilment some Divine act of self-revelation.

Given that Tillich requires a secure basis for the claim that human beings *as such* (as distinct from human beings living under certain specifiable social or cultural conditions) engage in the religious quest, it is not surprising that he should look with favour on the suggestion that the features of the human situation which give rise to this quest, far from being temporary and, in principle, eliminable features of the human situation, are necessary conditions of the very existence of human beings. Now to the question: 'How does Tillich propose to identify the features of the human situation which are necessary conditions of the existence of human beings and *a fortiori* ineliminable by human effort?' the answer seems to be: by refusing to draw any distinction between the features which are necessary conditions of human existence and the features which are necessary conditions of existence as such. Anything that can plausibly be represented as a necessary feature of the existence of human beings can equally, on this view, be represented as a necessary condition of the existence of all other beings. No clear distinction can be drawn, in short, between philosophical anthropology and ontology: the 'analysis of the human situation' undertaken by the philosopher in the interest of the adequate formulation of 'existential questions' yields the sort of doctrine of man which is also a doctrine of being or existence as such.

To sum up. Tillich's programme for a philosophical theology which will provide an alternative both to traditional 'theologies of revelation' and to traditional 'natural theologies' involves use of the 'method of correlation'. Examination of this method and of the central doctrines presented in the 'question-developing' parts of his theological system has shown that the philosopher is expected by Tillich to make his contribution to the construction of such a system in the form of a doctrine of man. This doctrine, however, has the peculiar property of also embodying an answer to the ontological question, the question concerning the nature of being or existence as such: it has this property because the obliteration of the distinction between philosophical anthropology and ontology seems to Tillich to be the indispensable means both of ensuring the possibility of the ontological enterprise and of providing a firm ground for the distinction between the religious

Philosophical Anthropology

and the non-religious needs of human beings. The extent of Tillich's failure either consistently to advocate or consistently to employ the method of correlation which he represents as the distinguishing characteristic of his own philosophical theology will be discussed in the next chapter.

Chapter 3

ONTOLOGY AND THEOLOGY

It is the purpose of this chapter to establish that there are passages in which Tillich conceives of ontology as a sort of philosophical theology. It must be made clear at the outset consequently in which of the several senses of 'theology' to be found in Tillich's writings he obliterates the distinction between 'theology' and ontology. It will be sufficient for this purpose to distinguish three ways in which Tillich uses this term. (1) 'Theology' is often used interchangeably with 'systematic theology'. It is being used in this way when Tillich maintains that the theologian ought to make use of the 'method of correlation'. (2) There is a *broader* sense of 'theology' in which it is the name of that discipline of which 'systematic theology' ('theology' in the first sense) is but one branch—the other branches being 'historical theology' and 'practical theology'.[1] (3) There is also a *narrower* use in which 'theology' is but one element in 'systematic theology'—the other major element being philosophy'. Thus, while in the second sense of 'theology' the 'historical theologian' or the 'practical theologian' is as much a 'theologian' as the 'systematic theologian', in the first sense it is the 'systematic theologian', to the exclusion of the 'historical theologian' and the 'practical theologian', who is, strictly speaking, charged with a 'theological' task, while in the third sense of 'theology' even the 'systematic theologian' is doing 'theology' only when he is not doing 'philosophy'.

[1] Tillich, *Systematic Theology* (Vol. I), pp. 32–8.

Ontology and Theology

It is the third of these uses of 'theology' which is important to the argument of this chapter. The method of correlation, as has been noted,[2] seems to require (a) that the theological element in Tillich's system be a doctrine of God and the philosophical element a doctrine of man; it seems to require, moreover, (b) that the doctrine of God be grounded in revelation and that the doctrine of man commend itself quite independently of revelation. It will be the argument of this chapter that, despite the demands of the method of correlation, there is a powerful strand in Tillich's thought which blurs the distinction between philosophy and theology by violating the second of these requirements.

Now there are (at least) two ways in which this second requirement might be violated—and the line between the philosophical and theological parts of Tillich's system obliterated accordingly. On the one hand, the theologian might be permitted to shape, on the basis of revelation, the doctrine of man to be utilised in the system. On the other hand, the philosopher might be permitted to frame a doctrine of God independently of revelation.

To hold that the distinction between philosophy and theology in Tillich's system is obliterated in the first of these ways is tantamount to a denial that his systematic theology is a philosophical theology at all: for on this view the philosopher is not only denied an opportunity to speculate about the existence and nature of God but is also robbed in practice of the right to contribute a doctrine of man to the system. That Tillich's performance as a systematic theologian accords with some such view as this has been maintained by at least one recent critic of his work: Bernard Martin has argued [3] that some parts of his doctrine of man, and in particular his doctrine of estrangement, are patent reformulations of a specifically Christian view of man.

To hold that the distinction between philosophy and theology in Tillich's system is obliterated in the second way indicated is

---

[2] See Chapter 2.
[3] In Martin, *The Existentialist Theology of Paul Tillich*.

Paul Tillich

tantamount to claiming that his systematic theology is a *purely* philosophical theology, a theology, that is, which owes nothing (except *per accidens*) to his understanding of the Christian revelation: for on this view not only is it the philosopher's task to elaborate a doctrine of man but it is also within his competence to speculate about the nature of God.

Since our interest is in the various ways in which Tillich conceives of the philosophical (or ontological) question, I shall be concerned in this chapter with that conception of systematic theology which enlarges, rather than with that which virtually eliminates, the philosopher's task in relation to systematic theology. And in particular I shall be concerned with the question whether Tillich does in fact so enlarge his conception of the ontologist's task as to permit him to speculate about the nature and existence of God. I shall argue that, in violation of the restrictions imposed by the method of correlation and despite his strictures against 'natural theology', Tillich does in fact invest the philosopher (or ontologist) with responsibility for the elaboration, independently of revelation, of a doctrine of God. I shall first examine the argument of Tillich's *Biblical Religion and the Search for Ultimate Reality*, in which an attempt is made by Tillich to work out the relation between ontology and theology. It will be shown that the 'synthesis' of ontology and theology which Tillich tries to achieve requires, not a mere *correlation* of ontology and theology (in the sense of 'correlation' discussed in Chapter 2) but their virtual *identification*. Secondly, I shall consider Tillich's criticisms of the proofs of the existence of God—which form the 'core', in his view, of 'natural theology' —with a view to establishing that far from entailing that it is impossible for the philosopher working independently of revelation to frame a doctrine of God, these criticisms actually presuppose just such a philosophical doctrine of God. Finally, I shall cite some of the evidence for Tillich's subscription to the view that the ontologist has available a means of ascertaining the nature of God without any appeal to revelation.

Ontology and Theology

I GOD AND BEING-ITSELF

Since it is one of Tillich's most emphatic and oft-repeated claims that the only non-symbolic assertion that can be made about God is that God is 'being-itself',[4] it might be thought that the question whether Tillich ever identifies the ontological question with the theological question ('the question of God') could be settled by enquiring whether the ontological question is ever described as a question about 'being-itself'. If the question could be settled in this way, then Tillich would certainly have to be regarded as guilty of identifying ontology with theology: for he frequently refers to the ontological question in this way.[5]

However, while Tillich's frequent characterisation of the ontological question as a question about 'being-itself' provides valuable evidence in support of the contention that he sometimes identifies ontology with theology, it is not by itself conclusive evidence. For some of the passages in which the ontological question is described as a question about 'being-itself' are passages in which it is quite clear that the ontological question is a question about the meaning of the verb 'to be' [6]—and it is not at all clear that to be interested in the meaning of the verb 'to be' is *ipso facto* to be interested in the 'question of God'. To distinguish *this* question about 'being-itself' from that other question about 'being-itself' which is the 'question of God' (and this latter question about 'being-itself' is the 'question of God' in virtue of Tillich's identification of 'God' with 'being-itself') is, of course, to draw attention to an ambiguity in Tillich's use of 'being-itself'. It is, however, an ambiguity of which Tillich is aware: in 'Reply to my Critics' he distinguishes between the sense of 'being-itself' in which to ask about 'being-itself' is to ask about the meaning of the verb 'to be' and the sense of 'being-itself' in which to ask about 'being-itself' is to ask about God.[7]

---

[4] *Systematic Theology* (Vol. I), pp. 264–5.
[5] 'The ontological question is: what is being-itself?' (*Systematic Theology* (Vol. I), p. 181; also *Biblical Religion and the Search for Ultimate Reality*, p. 13 and *passim*).
[6] See *Systematic Theology* (Vol. I), p. 181, for example. For further discussion of this version of the ontological question, see Chapter 5.
[7] 'Reply to my Critics', in Kegley and Bretall, *Theology of Paul Tillich*, p. 335.

Paul Tillich

However, examination of the contexts in which the ontological question is characterised as a question about 'being-itself' makes it clear that on at least some of these occasions it is not at all plausible to distinguish between the 'being-itself' about which the ontologist asks and the 'being-itself' which Tillich is prepared to identify with God. I propose to try to establish this by considering the characterisation of the ontological question as a question about 'being-itself' in *Biblical Religion and the Search for Ultimate Reality*.

There are at least two ways of lending weight to the contention that in *Biblical Religion and the Search for Ultimate Reality* the ontological question is really being identified by Tillich with the 'question of God'. To explain the first of these it is necessary to recall that in the opening part of this book Tillich tends to confuse the ontological question with the religious quest.[8] Now the most straightforward way (though not, as has already been noted [9] the only way) of simultaneously extricating Tillich from this confusion and accounting plausibly for his falling victim to it is to suppose that he really intends the ontological question to be regarded as a question about the object of the religious quest. Now since what man *qua* man seeks (according to *Biblical Religion and the Search for Ultimate Reality*) is 'ultimate reality'—or 'power of being', or 'being-itself'—the ontological question has to be represented as a question about 'ultimate reality'—or 'power of being', or 'being-itself'. But the 'being-itself' about which the ontologist asks must, then, be the 'being-itself' which Tillich is prepared to identify with 'God': for *qua* object of the religious quest 'being-itself' is man's 'ultimate concern' and 'God' is for Tillich simply the religious name for what concerns man ultimately.

But there is another, and more conclusive, way of showing that the ontological question described in *Biblical Religion and the Search for Ultimate Reality* as a question about 'being-itself' is none other than the 'question of God': this is to examine the

[8] See Chapter 1.
[9] Chapter 1, Section III.

main argument of the book with a view to establishing that Tillich's whole strategy in dealing with the central problem presupposes that these questions are identical.

The central problem in *Biblical Religion and the Search for Ultimate Reality* is the *prima facie* incompatibility of the ontological statements made by Tillich in his theological work (and here I am using 'theological' in the first of the three senses earlier distinguished—i.e. to denote all the work done by Tillich in his capacity as a systematic theologian) and the credal formulae which purport to articulate the dogmatic content of biblical religion.

In Chapters 3, 4 and 5 of *Biblical Religion and the Search for Ultimate Reality*, Tillich elaborates systematically the contrast between 'the doctrinal contents of biblical faith' and the 'conceptual forms of ontological thought'. First, he shows that whereas biblical religion presupposes that God is a person, and *a fortiori* a being, 'the ontological question asks the question of being itself, of the power of being in and above all beings'. Secondly, he shows that whereas the relation between man and God, according to biblical religion, is a reciprocal, person-to-person relation, the ontologist conceives of the relation between man and being-itself as a relation of 'participation'; and whereas ontological participation gives immediate awareness of something of which we are a part or which is a part of us, knowledge of God is possible, according to biblical religion, only if and to the extent that God is prepared to reveal himself to man. These contrasts are so sharp that Tillich is constrained to conclude this part of his survey of the relation between ontology and biblical theology on a pessimistic note: 'the confrontations of biblical religion and its personalism with the impersonalism of ontology seem to rule out any attempt at a synthesis.'

Now what is remarkable about Tillich's argument in these chapters is the assumption made throughout that the ontologist, in so far as he is interested in the question of being-itself, propounds theses about being-itself which are *prima facie* in conflict with the doctrine of God presupposed by biblical religion. The

Paul Tillich

ontologist's claim that 'being-itself' is not a being at all (and therefore, *a fortiori*, not a person) would not be incompatible (even *prima facie*) with the biblical theologian's claim that God is a person (and therefore, *a fortiori*, a being), if the 'being-itself' of which the ontologist speaks were not thought to be identical with the 'God' of whom the biblical theologian speaks. Again, the ontologist's claim that man 'participates in' and therefore has 'immediate awareness of' being-itself would not tend to undermine the biblical theologian's claim that knowledge of God is based on God's revelation of Himself to particular individuals in a person-to-person encounter, if it were not for the assumption that the God of biblical theology is identical with the 'being-itself' of ontology.

Since the positions contrasted in chapters 3, 4 and 5 are straightforwardly incompatible with one another only on the assumption that the God of the theologians is identical with the 'being-itself' of the ontologists, it might have been expected that Tillich would try to reconcile these positions by drawing attention to the falsity of this assumption. This would have been in harmony, moreover, with his claim that in a systematic theology constructed in accordance with the demands of the method of correlation there can be neither any synthesis of, nor any conflict between, philosophy and theology: philosophy and theology lack that 'common basis' which is a condition both of any synthesis of philosophy and theology and of any conflict between them.[10] Tillich's strategy in *Biblical Religion and the Search for Ultimate Reality*, however, consists rather in attempting to 'synthesise' the positions contrasted in Chapters 3, 4 and 5. 'Since the breakdown of the great synthesis between Christianity and the modern

---

[10] '... Is there a necessary conflict between the two [i.e. between theology and philosophy] and is there a possible synthesis between them? Both questions must be answered negatively. Neither is a conflict between them necessary, nor is a synthesis between them possible. A conflict presupposes a common basis on which to fight. But there is no common basis between theology and philosophy. If the theologian and the philosopher fight, they do so either on a philosophical or on a theological basis ... Thus there is no conflict between theology and philosophy, and there is no synthesis either—for exactly the same reason which ensures that there will be no conflict. A common basis is lacking.' (*Systematic Theology* (Vol. I), pp. 30-1).

Ontology and Theology

mind as attempted by Schleiermacher, Hegel, and nineteenth-century liberalism, an attitude of weariness has gripped the minds of people who are unable to accept one or other alternative.' (The alternatives to which Tillich is referring are, on the one hand, rejection of biblical religion in the name of ontology, and, on the other, rejection of ontology in the name of biblical religion.) 'They are too disappointed', Tillich continues, 'to try another synthesis after so many have failed. But there is no choice for us. We must try again!' [11]

Now despite the fact that Tillich (in the Introduction to *Systematic Theology*) links his denial of the possibility of 'synthesis' of philosophy and theology with the claim that they lack any 'common basis' the mere fact that in *Biblical Religion and the Search for Ultimate Reality* Tillich is prepared to insist that harmonisation of the positions contrasted (in Chapters 3, 4 and 5) must assume the form of 'synthesis' of these positions does not suffice to establish that the question of 'being-itself' is being regarded as identical with the question of God. For not only is there a passage in *Biblical Religion and the Search for Ultimate Reality* [12] in which 'synthesis' is used in just the way in which 'correlation' is used in the Introduction to *Systematic Theology*; there is even a reference—on the last page of the book—to 'the *correlation* of ontology and biblical religion', where the context makes it quite clear that Tillich is *not* drawing any distinction between 'correlation' and 'synthesis'.[13]

However, examination of the way in which Tillich attempts,

---

[11] Tillich, *Biblical Religion and the Search for Ultimate Reality*, p. 57.

[12] *Ibid.*, p. 42. In this passage Tillich first draws attention to the *prima facie* impossibility of any 'synthesis' of the theological and philosophical positions contrasted in Chapters 3, 4 and 5, and then continues: 'It will be the task of a part of the following chapter and of the last to show ... that each side [i.e. each of ontology and biblical theology] needs the other for its own realisation. But this relation is by no means to be found on the surface. It is necessary to penetrate deeply into both the nature of biblical religion and the nature of ontology in order to discover their profound *interdependence*.' (My italics.) 'Interdependence' is one of the words used by Tillich to describe the nature of the relation between the philosophical and the theological halves of a system constructed in accordance with the demands of the method of correlation (see *Systematic Theology* (Vol. II), pp. 14–18, e.g.).

[13] *Ibid.*, p. 85.

65

Paul Tillich

in the final chapter of *Biblical Religion and the Search for Ultimate Reality*, to 'synthesise' the positions he has contrasted in Chapters 3, 4 and 5 makes it quite clear that 'synthesis' does *not* involve the sort of correlation of these positions which would represent them as compatible because they embody solutions to *different*, though related, problems—although this is the only sort of 'synthesis' of ontological and theological doctrines loyal adherence to the method of correlation would permit. To 'synthesise' these positions is, on the contrary, to show that despite the fact that they embody solutions to a *common* problem, they are not in fact incompatible with one another when they are correctly understood—simply because, when correctly understood, they can be seen not to differ in anything but formulation.

Thus, in discussing the opposition between the view that God is *a* being (which is implied by the biblical view that God is *a* person) and the ontological thesis that being-itself is not *a* being at all, Tillich tries to show that there are elements in biblical religion which require the doctrine that God is personal to be reinterpreted in a way which eliminates the conflict between this doctrine and the ontological thesis. A 'synthesis' of the ostensibly incompatible ontological and theological doctrines is to be achieved, it would appear, by representing the latter, when suitably reinterpreted, as *identical* with the former. Again, in discussing the opposition between the view that the relation between man and God (actualised, say, in prayer) is a person-to-person relation and the ontological thesis that the relation between man and 'being-itself' is one of 'participation', Tillich tries to show that there are elements in biblical religion which require the doctrine that the 'divine-human' relation is a personal one to be reinterpreted in a way which eliminates the contradiction between this doctrine and the ontologist's claim that man 'participates' in being-itself. 'In every true prayer God is both he to whom we pray and he who prays through us.' [14] Here too, the desired harmonisation of ostensibly incompatible doctrines is apparently to be achieved by reinterpreting one of them (the

[14] *Ibid.*, p. 81.

Ontology and Theology

theological doctrine) until it coincides with the other (the ontological doctrine). Finally, in discussing the opposition between the biblical doctrine that knowledge of God is grounded in God's revelation of himself to individuals in something like a person-to-person encounter and the ontological thesis that in virtue of his 'participation' in being-itself man has an 'immediate awareness' of being-itself, Tillich tries to show that there is an important strand in biblical theology which requires that God's self-revelation be thought of as 'God manifesting himself to himself' rather than as 'a conversation between two beings'.[15] By reinterpreting the Christian doctrine of revelation in this way, Tillich hopes to be able to diminish the difference between it and the ontological doctrine that 'immediate experience' is the source of knowledge of being-itself.

Now harmonisation of the *prima facie* incompatible positions contrasted in Chapters 3, 4 and 5 *could* not take the form of the sort of 'synthesis' of these positions Tillich clearly tries to achieve in the last chapter of the book were it not being taken for granted that the 'being-itself', about which the ontological theses he considers are propounded, is *identical* with the God of biblical theology. Tillich's whole strategy, then, in dealing with the central problem of *Biblical Religion and the Search for Ultimate Reality*—a problem generated by the *prima facie* incompatibility of certain ontological doctrines with certain theological doctrines—seems to require that the ontological question, when formulated as a question about being-itself, be *identified* with the theological question, 'the question of God'. It is not surprising, consequently, that Tillich should conclude his discussion of the relation between ontology and biblical theology by rejecting Pascal's dictum about the God of the philosophers not being the God of Abraham, Isaac and Jacob. '*Against* Pascal I say', writes Tillich, 'the God of Abraham, Isaac and Jacob and the God of the philosophers is the same God.'[16]

---

[15] *Ibid.*, p. 78.
[16] *Ibid.*, p. 85.

Paul Tillich

11 TILLICH'S CRITICISMS OF THE ARGUMENTS FOR THE EXISTENCE OF GOD

It was noted in the last chapter that Tillich, when discussing the method of correlation employed in his system, contrasts his own procedure as a systematic theologian with 'three inadequate methods of relating the contents of the Christian faith to man's spiritual experience'. The first of these methods, the 'supranaturalistic', takes 'the Christian message to be a sum of revealed truths which have fallen into the human situation like strange bodies from a strange world'. The second, the 'humanistic' or 'naturalistic', 'derives the Christian message from man's natural state', explaining the contents of the Christian faith as 'creations of man's religious self-realisation in the progressive process of religious history'. The third method, the 'dualistic' (so named because it 'builds a supernatural structure on a natural substructure') posits a 'body of theological truths which man can reach through his own efforts'. It is the task of 'natural theology', according to the protagonists of the third method, to articulate this 'body of theological truth', and it is the so-called 'arguments for the existence of God' which are, according to Tillich, the most important part of natural theology in this sense. Tillich represents his own procedure as a philosophical theologian as differing from that of the sort of philosophical theologian who is a 'natural theologian' in that he thinks it is not within the competence of the philosopher to enunciate propositions about God, though it *is* an important part of his task to formulate those questions to which propositions about God—made, however, on the basis of revelation—provide possible answers.

I want in this section to examine Tillich's criticisms of the traditional theistic proofs in order to determine whether his break with 'natural theology' is as decisive as it would be if he were content to use the method of correlation described in the last chapter.

Tillich claims to have two objections to the traditional theistic proofs. 'There can be little doubt that the arguments are a failure

Ontology and Theology

in so far as they claim to be arguments. Both the concept of existence and the method of arguing to a conclusion are inadequate to the idea of God.'[17]

Although Tillich no doubt supposes that the proposition 'God exists' does not follow from any set of non-theological propositions (that is, from any set of propositions which does not include at least one proposition about God), it is not on this ground that he rejects the theistic proofs. The point of the first of Tillich's criticisms—viz. that 'the concept of existence' is 'inadequate to the idea of God'—is clearly to draw attention to the unsatisfactoriness of the proposition which is the conclusion of the theistic proofs. The proposition 'God exists' is unsatisfactory because it is held by Tillich to be self-contradictory.

> 'However it be defined, the "existence of God" contradicts the idea of a creative ground of essence and existence. The ground of being cannot be found within the totality of beings, nor can the ground of essence and existence participate in the tensions and disruptions characteristic of the transition from essence to existence.'[18]

The proposition 'God exists' is self-contradictory because (a) God is, according to Tillich, 'being-itself', where 'being-itself' is emphatically *not a* being 'alongside' (or 'above', for that matter) other beings, and because (b) 'existence' can only be predicated of 'beings'.

Now a criticism of this first sort could be levelled against the proposition 'God exists' even if it were *not* represented (by natural theologians) as the conclusion of an argument. Consequently, this first criticism is not really a criticism of the *arguments* for the existence of God.

Tillich's second criticism seems to differ from the first in that it embodies, *prima facie*, an objection to these arguments *qua* arguments. Yet even here, Tillich does not try to establish that the proposition 'God exists' does not follow from some set of

---

[17] *Systematic Theology* (Vol. I), p. 227.
[18] *Ibid.*, p. 227.

Paul Tillich

propositions about the world. What he tries to establish is that 'the method of arguing to a conclusion contradicts the idea of God'. 'Every argument derives conclusions from something that is given about something that is sought. In arguments for the existence of God the world is given and God is sought. Some characteristics of the world make the conclusion "God" necessary. God is derived from the world.' [19]

Now it might be thought that Tillich supposes that the whole enterprise of trying to derive propositions about God from propositions about the world 'contradicts the idea of God' simply because the God whose existence might be established in this way would be 'dependent on the world'; and of course a God who was 'dependent on the world'—who depended for his existence upon the existence of the world—would not be 'God'. But this is not Tillich's reason for claiming that the 'method of arguing to a conclusion contradicts the idea of God'. He recognises, with Aquinas, that it is one thing to derive propositions about God from propositions about the world, and quite another to hold that God depends for his very existence upon the world. Propositions about God might well be logically dependent on propositions about the world, without it being the case that God is himself dependent upon the world for his existence. 'Thomas Aquinas is correct when . . . he asserts that what is first in itself may be last for our knowledge.' [20]

But although a God whose existence is inferred from some set of propositions about the world need not be *dependent* for his existence on the world, any such God must (according to Tillich) be a mere *part* of the world. 'If we derive God from the world, he cannot be that which transcends the world infinitely. He is the "missing link" discovered by correct conclusions. . . . God is "world", a missing part of that from which he is derived in terms of conclusions.' [21] Now to represent God as 'part of the world' is to represent him as *a* being alongside the other

[19] *Ibid.*, p. 228.
[20] *Ibid.*, p. 228.
[21] *Ibid.*, p. 228.

Ontology and Theology

beings which make up the world—and in Tillich's eyes such a conception of God is 'inadequate'. Thus, Tillich is able to maintain that 'the method of arguing to a conclusion is inadequate to the idea of God'—and this is his second criticism of the traditional arguments for the existence of God—only because he thinks he can represent the adherence of natural theologians to the 'inadequate' conception of God as *a* being as a consequence of their attempt to construct *arguments* in support of statements about God. There is, he thinks, a necessary connection between the view that such arguments can be constructed and the view that God is *a* being.

This second objection of Tillich's to the traditional theistic proofs invites two comments.

There appears to be no incompatibility between the claim that propositions about God are derivable from propositions about the world and the claim that God is misconceived if he is thought of as *a* being 'alongside' (or 'above') other beings. Tillich is mistaken, consequently, in linking the subscription of natural theologians to what he regards as an inadequate view of God (viz. the view that God is to be conceived of as *a* being [22]) with their claim that certain propositions about God can be derived from propositions about the world. The inadequacy of the traditional conception of God as *a* being—if inadequate it be—cannot be attributed even in part to the fact that an attempt has been made by natural theologians to establish *by means of argument* the truth of certain propositions about him.

Secondly, given Tillich's characterisation of the theistic proofs as attempts to derive 'God' from the 'world', the 'world' being 'given', 'God' what is 'sought',[23] it is simply false that any

---

[22] I take no issue with Tillich's claim that natural theologians have traditionally subscribed to this—allegedly inadequate—conception of God. Whether they have or not seems to depend on one's view of the denotation of the expression 'natural theologian': if Spinoza were to qualify as a 'natural theologian', for example, the claim would be false.

[23] *Systematic Theology* (Vol. I), p. 228. Although Tillich claims to be offering in this passage a brief account of what is common to the structure of *all* the arguments for the existence of God, the account fits what he later distinguishes as 'the cosmological argument' better than it fits 'the so-called ontological argument'.

Paul Tillich

God whose existence is derived from propositions about the world is part of the world. For when Tillich says that in the theistic proofs the 'world' is *given* and God *sought*, he is so using the word 'world' that God is *not* part of the 'world'. If, *per impossibile*, God *were* part of the 'world' in the sense intended in this passage, then God too would be *given* and would therefore not need to be *sought*: there would, accordingly, be no need for *proofs* of the existence of God. Now if it is false that any God whose existence is 'derived' from the 'world' is part of the world from which his existence has been derived, then the question whether his being part of the world is a function of the fact that an attempt has been made to *argue* for his existence is a question which *cannot* arise.

It is open to Tillich, of course, to argue that any God whose existence is derived from the world must needs be *a* being (since existence is predicated of him in the conclusion of such a proof and since existence can be predicated only of *beings*) and that he is *therefore* part of the world. It is apparent, however, that this involves a use of 'world' different from that employed in Tillich's brief description of the theistic proofs: the 'world', in the sense *now* in question, cannot be what is said to be 'given' in the theistic proofs precisely because it contains what is said to be 'sought' (as *distinct* from 'given') in the theistic proofs. Moreover, God's being a mere part of the world (in this new sense of 'world') is an inference from the proposition that he is *a* being, and this proposition in turn is inferred from the fact that existence is predicated of God in the conclusion of the theistic proofs; whereas, in his presentation of his second criticism of the theistic proofs, Tillich represents God's being a mere part of the world as an implication of the attempt made by natural theologians to derive propositions about him from propositions about the world. It is *not*, then, the 'method of arguing to a conclusion' which is 'inadequate to the idea of God' but the attribution of existence to God in the conclusion of the theistic proofs.

If my view of Tillich's second criticism of the traditional

Ontology and Theology

theistic proofs is correct, Tillich has only one objection to these proofs: viz. that the conclusion they are designed to establish is unsatisfactory, because self-contradictory. Now the interesting thing about this criticism is that Tillich objects on *ontological* grounds to the claim that God is *a* being. It is in the strength of the claim that God is *being-itself* that Tillich rejects the traditional theistic conception of God as *a* being. Consequently, not only is there nothing in Tillich's treatment of the traditional proofs of the existence of God to suggest either that he thinks it is in principle impossible for the ontologist (as distinct from the theologian who has access to 'revelatory' sources) to make statements about God or that he thinks it is in principle impossible for the ontologist to construct arguments designed to prove such statements, but the only reason he gives for objecting to these proofs seems to presuppose the possibility of the ontologist's *making* (quite independently of revelation) certain statements about God, such statements as that God is not *a* being, or that God is 'being-itself'.

III IMMEDIATE AWARENESS OF GOD

That Tillich should not be averse to making statements about God in his capacity as ontologist (and that therefore, despite his professed opposition to 'natural theology', he is himself a natural theologian of a sort) may be confirmed by an examination of Tillich's attempt to rehabilitate the ontological argument for the existence of God. 'The ontological argument in its various forms gives a description of the way in which potential infinity is present in actual finitude. As far as the description goes, that is, so far as it is analysis and not argument, it is valid.' The ontological argument, Tillich seems to be arguing, can be understood as an attempt to analyse 'human finitude' with a view to exhibiting the possibility of 'the question of God which is implied in human finitude'. What, then, is it which facilitates the asking of the question of God? Not simply, as one would expect, man's experience of what it means to be a finite being; rather, it is man's 'awareness of the infinite', his 'awareness of

Paul Tillich

God'. 'The question of God is possible because an awareness of God is present in the question of God.' [24] Had Tillich been content to claim that human beings *qua* aware of their finitude form some *conception* of God (as, e.g. capable of overcoming the threat of nonbeing which is implicit in their finitude) and are therefore in a position to ask the question of God, his reinterpretation of the ontological argument might well have been regarded (as he himself wishes it to be) as consisting in the sort of analysis of 'human finitude' which shows how human beings, *qua* conscious of their finitude and what it implies, are receptive to a revelatory answer to the question of God. But if human beings have an 'immediate awareness' of God, and if it is this 'immediate awareness' which facilitates the asking of the question of God, can it reasonably be claimed that it is outwith the ontologist's competence to make *any* assertion about God? There is surely a connection between Tillich's characterisation of God as 'being-itself' (and the complementary refusal to tolerate the suggestion that God is *a* being) and the claim that human beings are 'immediately aware' of God: it is surely *because* the God disclosed in this 'immediate awareness' is held by Tillich *not* to be *a* being at all that Tillich is able to claim that God is 'being-itself'. Nor is Tillich unprepared to make statements about what is disclosed in this 'immediate awareness'. In his 'Two Types of Philosophy of Religion', for example, where he discusses at length the nature of what he calls 'man's ontological awareness of the Unconditional', it is made clear that the 'Unconditional' of which there is 'immediate awareness' is precisely *not a* being but 'the *prius* of everything that has being'. 'Being itself, as present in the ontological awareness, is power of Being but not the most powerful being.' [25]

Now if there is such a thing as immediate awareness of God, and if Tillich is prepared to assert that the God disclosed in this immediate awareness is 'being-itself' and not *a* being, then it is understandable not only why Tillich should object to the

[24] *Ibid.* (Vol. I), pp. 228–9.
[25] Tillich, *Theology of Culture*, pp. 25–6.

Ontology and Theology

conclusion of the theistic proofs, but also why he should be opposed to the whole enterprise of *deriving* propositions about God from non-theological premises. The proposition 'God exists' will be unsatisfactory because the God of whom man is immediately aware is not *a* being at all. And if propositions about God can be made on the basis of 'immediate experience' then it is altogether unnecessary for the philosophical theologian to search for non-theological premises from which to derive propositions about God.

But equally, if there is such a thing as immediate awareness of God, and if Tillich is prepared to assert that the God disclosed in this awareness is 'being-itself', it is not at all clear that his own procedure as a philosophical theologian differs as radically as he claims from the procedure of the 'natural theologian'. For even if, unlike the traditional natural theologian, he does not conceive of God as *a* being, and even if, again unlike the traditional natural theologian, he thinks it is unnecessary for non-theological propositions to be adduced in support of propositions about God, he seems to resemble the natural theologian in what is, after all, the crucial respect: viz. in his preparedness to *make* statements about God in his capacity as a philosopher, such statements as that 'God is being-itself' and that 'God is not *a* being'. If Tillich were consistent in his declared opposition to the *method* employed by natural theologians he would be committed to holding that *all* propositions about God (that is, all answers to 'the question of God') are made on the basis of revelation. Yet it is clear from his criticisms of the theistic proofs no less than from his frequent identification of the ontological question with the question about 'being-itself' (i.e. with 'the question of God') that he is committed *as an ontologist* to the making of statements about God. And a means of making such statements which involves no appeal to revelation seems to be put within the ontologist's reach by Tillich's conviction that human beings have an 'immediate awareness' of God.

Chapter 4

THE CONDITIONS OF EXPERIENCE

'The suggestion made here is to call philosophy that cognitive approach to reality in which reality as such is the object. Reality as such, or reality as a whole, is not the whole of reality; it is the structure which makes reality a whole and therefore a potential object of knowledge. Inquiring into the nature of reality as such means inquiring into those structures, categories, and concepts which are presupposed in the cognitive encounter with every realm of reality ... The question regarding the character of the general structures which make experience possible is always the same. It is *the* philosophical question.' [1]

'Metaphysics should be defined as the analysis of those elements in the encountered reality which belong to its general structure and make experience universally possible.' [2]

The most noteworthy feature of these definitions of philosophy is that while they agree in ascribing to the philosopher an interest in the elucidation of the 'structure of being' (or 'reality'), they trace this interest to the fact that it is the 'structure of being' which *makes experience possible* rather than to a desire to identify the features of the human situation which give rise to the religious quest [3] or to a desire to give some account of the meaning of the

---

[1] Tillich, *Systematic Theology* (Vol. I), p. 22.
[2] Tillich, 'The Relation of Metaphysics and Theology', *Review of Metaphysics* (1956), p. 57.
[3] See Chapter 1.

The Conditions of Experience

verb 'to be' [4] or to a desire to illumine the 'mystery of being' by explaining why there is a world at all.[5]

However, the account of the philosopher's task they provide is ambiguous, for the claim that the philosopher should investigate the structure of being with a view to throwing light on the conditions of the possibility of experience is construed by Tillich in two quite different ways.

On the one hand, the conditions of the possibility of experience are identified with certain features of the *objects* of experience—features they must (allegedly) have in order to be possible objects of experience. On this view it is taken for granted that the 'structure' which makes experience possible informs all the things which are 'encounterable' by the human mind: were it not for this 'structure' it would not be possible for them to be experienced at all. 'From the time of Parmenides it has been a common assumption of all philosophers that the *logos*, the word which grasps and shapes reality, can do so only because reality itself has a *logos* character.' [6] Experience is possible only because reality has a certain structure, the sort of structure which makes it possible for the mind to 'grasp' it. And it is this structure which it is the job of the ontologist to articulate.

On the second interpretation of Tillich's question, it concerns, not the features of the things we experience which alone enable them to be experienced by us, but the nature of the distinction between the experiencing subject and what he experiences: for experience to be possible at all, the distinction between experiencing subject and experienced object must, it is held, be grounded in an ontological distinction between the 'self' and its 'world'.

I THE OBJECTS OF EXPERIENCE AND
THE STRUCTURE OF BEING

To hold that the ontological question is a question about the conditions of the possibility of experience (on the first interpretation of this question) is to make two distinguishable claims:

[4] See Chapter 5.
[5] See Chapter 6.
[6] *Systematic Theology* (Vol. I), p. 83.

Paul Tillich

first, that certain features of the things we experience make it possible for them to be experienced; secondly, that these features constitute 'the structure of being'. Tillich may consequently be attacked either on the ground that he has not demonstrated the reasonableness of his question about what makes experience possible or on the ground that he has not established that this question is a question about the 'structure of being'. His position is vulnerable to both sorts of attack.

1. There are at least three ways in which the first of Tillich's claims—the claim that certain features of the things we experience make it possible for them to be experienced—might be misconstrued.

(a) When he claims that it is a condition of experience that 'reality' (*qua* object of experience) have a certain structure—the structure which it is the ontologist's task to describe—he might be thought to be asserting no more than that anything which is *actually* an object of experience must be such that it is *capable* of being an object of experience. In at least one place—in a passage in which he is trying to restate his doctrine of 'objective reason', according to which 'reality' *qua* object of experience must have the sort of rational structure which is a necessary condition of experience of it—he comes close to expressing his thesis in this trivial form. He writes: '... the world can be recognised because its structures and laws have the essential character of being intelligible.'[7] However, Tillich clearly could not make the claim that reality's having a certain structure is a condition of experience the basis of the further claim that it is the ontologist's task to describe this structure if the first of these claims could be reduced to the trivial (and apparently pointless) statement that what is actually an object of experience must be capable of being an object of experience!

(b) It might, alternatively, be thought that Tillich is claiming that if any particular object is to be experienced, it must have the 'structure' which makes it *that* particular object and no

[7] 'Reply to my Critics', in Kegley and Bretall, *Theology of Paul Tillich*, p. 333.

The Conditions of Experience

other. On this interpretation, *all* the features of the objects of experience would have to be represented as conditions of experience: for it takes *all* of these features to make the objects of experience *what* they are, and it is the conditions which must be fulfilled if *they* are to be experienced which the ontologist must try to discover. It is, however, clearly *not* Tillich's intention to assign to the ontologist the task of describing *all* the features of *all* the things which are experienced by human beings. For quite apart from the impossibility in principle of such a task, Tillich clearly assumes that it is *certain* features of the objects of experience to the exclusion of their other features which make it possible for them to be experienced.

(c) Finally it might be thought that Tillich is maintaining that it is a condition of the possibility of experience that the subject of experience be able to discriminate the various objects presented to him—where the 'structured-ness' of these objects is a necessary condition of the making of these indispensable judgments of discrimination. Tillich's, however, is a more specific claim than this: namely, that there are *certain* features of the objects of experience which are, to the exclusion of their other features, the *conditiones sine quibus non* of experience of these objects.

But if this is what Tillich's claim amounts to, it is exposed *prima facie* to the obvious objection that there is just no way of isolating these 'experience-facilitating' features. They certainly cannot be singled out by reference to the question whether they do or do not make it possible for the objects of experience to be experienced! What is needed, clearly, is some criterion for the identification of the 'experience-facilitating' characteristics of the objects of experience. But is any such criterion available?

There is a hint as to what Tillich takes this criterion to be in the passages quoted at the beginning of this chapter. 'The question regarding the character of the *general* structures that make experience possible is . . . *the* philosophical question.' [8] 'Metaphysics should be defined as the analysis of those elements in

[8] *Systematic Theology* (Vol. I), p. 22 (I have italicised 'general').

Paul Tillich

the encountered reality which belong to its *general* structure and make experience universally possible.'[9] Tillich hopes, it would seem, to be able to identify the structures which make experience possible by identifying the structures which are *common* to all objects of experience. A more explicit statement of this view is to be found in Tillich's discussion of the method of ontology in *Love, Power and Justice*. 'Ontology', Tillich writes, 'is analytical. It analyses the encountered reality . . . It separates those elements of the real which are generic or particular from those elements which are constitutive for everything that is and therefore are *universal*. . . . it elaborates the latter through critical analysis.'[10] The analysis of those 'elements of the real'—i.e. of 'the encountered reality'—which are 'universal' is the task of the ontologist. It is the 'universality' of certain 'elements' of the 'encountered reality' which marks them off from other features of the objects of experience as worthy of the attention of the ontologist.

Nor is it difficult to see why Tillich should suppose that the features of the things we experience which make them possible objects of experience are features they have in common. For given that the fact that something is an object of experience is held by Tillich to require an explanation in terms of its 'experience-facilitating' features, and given also that it is a *common* property of the things which are objects of experience—viz. their being objects of experience—which gives rise to the ontological question in this form, it is natural that Tillich should assume that the features of these things which make it possible for them to be experienced are features they have in common.

Natural, perhaps; but not, on that account, defensible. For there is, of course, no necessary connection between something's being a feature common to all the things we experience and its being an 'experience-facilitating' feature of these things (in some sense in which other, less 'universal' features of these things are not). Tillich's criterion for the identification of the 'experience-facilitating' features of the objects of experience does nothing, in

[9] 'The Relation of Metaphysics and Theology', p. 57 (my italics).
[10] Tillich, *Love, Power and Justice*, p. 23.

The Conditions of Experience

short, to remove any misgivings that may be felt in regard to the assumption that there are certain isolable features of the objects of experience which make it possible for them to be experienced. But although this assumption is in grave need of detailed elucidation and defence, neither is provided by Tillich.

2. Even if Tillich were more successful than he is in showing the reasonableness of an inquiry into the features of the objects of experience which make it possible for these objects to be experienced, that such an inquiry is identical with ontology would await demonstration. There is a special reason why their identity cannot be assumed. As has been noted in an earlier chapter (see Chapter 2, Section III, p. 52), Tillich's occasional doubts about the very possibility of ontology are grounded in his refusal to identify the beings into whose structure the ontologist is supposed to inquire with the objects of experience: yet now, it would appear, it is only by identifying these that he can hope to represent the ontological question as a question about what makes experience possible. The identity of these questions is, however, an assumed, and not a demonstrated, identity.

II THE DISTINCTION BETWEEN SUBJECT AND OBJECT AND THE STRUCTURE OF BEING

According to the alternative interpretation of Tillich's question about the 'structure' which 'makes experience possible', this 'structure' does not inform the objects of experience at all; rather it is the ground of the distinction between the experiencing subject and what he experiences.

This interpretation seems to be required by the answer Tillich gives to the ontological question when he propounds the doctrine of the 'basic ontological structure'. For the 'basic ontological structure' is the 'self-world structure' and as such *could not* be regarded as informing the objects of experience: to say that the objects of experience exhibit the 'self-world structure' is meaningless. A meaning can, however, be given to the claim that the 'self-world structure' is a condition of the possibility of experience

Paul Tillich

if this claim is represented as an attempt on Tillich's part to articulate the nature of the relation between the experiencing subject and what he experiences.

Now in maintaining that the 'basic ontological structure' is the 'self-world structure', Tillich is not asserting merely that it must be possible, in analysing an experience, to distinguish between the experiencing subject and the experienced object. The thesis in this form might after all be represented as a misleading formulation of the grammatical thesis that the verb 'to experience' is a transitive verb and that consequently it must be possible to locate, in sentences containing this verb, both a 'subject' and an 'object'. Tillich's primary contention, rather, is that the distinction between experiencing subject and experienced object is grounded in a fundamental ontological distinction, that between the 'self' and its 'world'. 'The subject-object structure', he writes (in one of the central passages in the first volume of *Systematic Theology*), 'presupposes the self-world structure as the basic articulation of being.' [11] Only by advancing this larger (even if somewhat enigmatic) claim, it would appear, could Tillich hope to render plausible the contention that the question about what makes experience possible (on the interpretation under consideration) is an ontological question.

I shall examine briefly the main ways in which Tillich attempts to substantiate this larger claim—in order to determine whether he succeeds in making plausible the related claim that the question about what makes experience possible is an ontological question. That the 'self-world structure' is what makes experience possible Tillich tries to establish in two ways: (a) by argument, and (b) by appeal to 'immediate experience'.

(a) In a preliminary reference to his doctrine of the basic ontological structure, Tillich says of it that it is 'the implicit condition of the ontological question'. He proceeds to elucidate this claim as follows: 'The ontological question presupposes an asking subject and an object about which the question is asked; it presupposes the subject-object structure of being, which in

[11] *Systematic Theology* (Vol. I), p. 183.

The Conditions of Experience

turn presupposes the self-world structure as the basic articulation of being.'[12]

This passage not only contains Tillich's answer to the ontological question in the form under consideration; it also embodies an argument in support of this answer. The answer, of course, is that the basic ontological structure which 'makes experience possible' is the 'self-world structure'. In the supporting argument[13] Tillich takes for granted that the ontological question is a legitimate question and then claims (1) that it is a condition of its legitimacy that a distinction can be drawn between the asker of the ontological question and that about which he asks (that is, between the asking 'subject' and the 'object' of his question), and (2) that this distinction between 'subject' and 'object' in turn presupposes (as a condition of its legitimacy) the further (ontological) distinction between the 'self' and its 'world'.

Tillich's argument here is seriously at odds with itself. (1) seems to require that the 'self-world structure' be represented as the 'object' of the ontological question—the 'object', that is, which is to be distinguished from the asker of the ontological question (the 'subject'). (*That* this is what (1) requires is inescapable given that the ontological question is a question about the basic ontological structure which 'makes experience possible' and given that this 'structure' *is* (according to Tillich) the 'self-world structure'.) (2) however, seems to require that the 'object' of the ontological question be identifiable, *not* with the 'self-world structure' *as a whole*, but with one of the 'elements' in the 'self-world structure'—viz. the 'world'. (*That* it is the 'world' and not the 'self-world structure' as a whole which must be

---

[12] *Ibid.*, pp. 182–3.
[13] A puzzling feature of this argument is its starting-point. If an answer is being sought to the ontological question *qua* question about the conditions of the possibility of *experience*, why does Tillich take a *question* as the starting-point of his argument and go on, consequently, to ask about the conditions of the possibility of this question? *Prima facie* it would have been more pertinent for him to have taken some putative *experience* (or perhaps some statement about experience) as the starting-point of his argument and then proceeded to determine the condition of *its* possibility. As it is, the precise connection between a statement about the conditions of the possibility of the ontological question and a statement about the conditions of the possibility of experience is left in some doubt.

identified with the 'object'-term of the 'subject-object structure' seems to be an implication of Tillich's preparedness to assert that 'the subject-object structure of being presupposes the self-world structure as the basic articulation of being': for to make this assertion *tout court*—that is, *without* giving some account of the special relation between the 'subject-object structure' and the 'self-world structure'—is surely to be committed to holding that 'subject' and 'object' are to be correlated with 'self' and 'world' respectively.[14] There is thus a lack of correspondence between the subject-object distinction said to be 'presupposed' by the ontological question and the subject-object distinction which is said to 'presuppose' the 'self-world structure as the basic articulation of being'. Yet for these (subject-object) distinctions to coincide is, of course, essential to the argument: their identity is the only link between (1) and (2), and it is only if there is such a link that Tillich can claim to have shown that the 'basic ontological structure' is the 'implicit condition of the ontological question'.[15]

Tillich's argument in support of the thesis that the 'basic ontological structure' is the 'self-world structure'—the argument that takes the legitimacy of the ontological question as its starting point—must, then, be held to be a failure. It cannot, consequently, be used either in support of the claim that the 'self-world structure' is what makes experience possible or in support of the (related) claim that the question about what makes experience possible is an *ontological* question.[16]

(b) Of the two claims which embody Tillich's argument in

[14] Cf. Tillich's statement that 'the "subject-object structure" is *rooted* in the self-world correlation ... and grows out of it' (*Systematic Theology* (Vol. I), p. 190); also the discussion of the distinction between 'subjective reason' and 'objective reason' (*Systematic Theology* (Vol. I), pp. 83–5); also the account of the relation between the 'self-world polarity' and the 'subject-object structure' (*Systematic Theology* (Vol. I), p. 190).
[15] *Systematic Theology* (Vol. I), p. 182.
[16] If it should be impossible to establish any satisfactory connection between Tillich's question about the conditions of the possibility of the ontological question and the question he claims is the ontological question (viz. the question about the conditions of the possibility of *experience*), then the argument discussed above could not be used to support any thesis about what makes *experience* possible *even if the argument were satisfactory*.

The Conditions of Experience

support of the thesis that it is the 'self-world structure' which makes experience possible, the first—that it is a condition of the legitimacy of the ontological question that it be possible to distinguish between the asker of the ontological question and that about which he asks—requires that the 'object' of this question be assumed to be the 'self-world structure'. In at least one passage,[17] however, Tillich warns against the supposition that the 'self-world structure' can be represented as an 'object'. 'The basic structure of being and all its elements ... lose their meaning and their truth if they are seen as objects among objects.' He maintains, moreover, that it is in *immediate experience* that the basic ontological structure (the structure which makes experience possible) is disclosed. 'Man is able to answer the ontological question himself because he experiences directly and immediately the structure of being and its elements ... Man is aware of the structures which make cognition possible ... They are immediately present to him.' Now the appeal to 'immediate experience' for an answer to the (ontological) question about the possibility of experience not only eliminates the need for (and perhaps also the possibility of) any *argument* in support of an answer to this question; it also renders inadmissible the claim (which plays so important a role in Tillich's argument) that the 'self-world structure' is representable as an 'object'. It is, after all, the fact that 'subject' and 'object' are *not* distinguishable elements within the experience to which appeal is here being encouraged which provides the warrant for the claim that this is an appeal to 'immediate experience'.

There are, however, at least three difficulties in the way of Tillich's appealing to 'immediate experience' in support of his answer to the question about what makes experience possible.

In the first place, the claim that what 'immediate experience' discloses is the 'self-world' (or 'subject-object') structure of being conflicts with the claim (usually made by Tillich in passages in which 'immediate experience' is discussed) that what 'immediate experience' discloses is not the 'self-world' (or 'subject-object')

[17] *Systematic Theology* (Vol. I), p. 187.

Paul Tillich

structure but something which 'underlies' or 'transcends' the split between 'subject' and 'object', between 'self' and 'world'. Consider the following passages:

> 'Like many other appeals to immediate experience, it (i.e. the thinking of the Existential thinker) is trying to find a level on which the contrast between "subject" and "object" has not arisen. It aims to cut under the "subject-object" distinction and to reach that stratum of Being which Jaspers, for instance, calls the "*Ursprung*" or "source".' [18]

> 'Man is immediately aware of something which is the *prius* of the separation and interaction of subject and object.' [19]

Secondly, it is difficult to see how 'immediate experience' *could* be the source of the ontologist's knowledge about the basic ontological structure—if it is the case *both* that 'immediate experience' is by definition the sort of experience within which 'subject' and 'object' ('self' and 'world') can *not* be distinguished, *and* that the basic ontological structure is the 'self-world structure'.

Thirdly, even if, *per impossibile*, the 'self-world structure' (or the 'subject-object structure') *were* disclosed in 'immediate experience' (and even if this structure were conceded to be the basic ontological structure), the thesis that this structure is *what makes experience possible* would not have been established thereby. To subscribe to this latter thesis on the basis of an appeal to 'immediate experience' would be to be committed to the acceptance of both of two incompatible propositions: (i) that within experiences of *all* kinds it is possible to distinguish between the 'subject' of the experience and the 'object' of the experience (i.e. between 'self' and 'world'), and (ii) that there is at least one kind of experience—viz. that in which there is immediate or direct

---

[18] *Theology of Culture*, p. 92. Although this passage is taken from an article describing 'Existential Philosophy', it is clear in the article that Tillich does not wish to dissociate himself from the only positive view which all Existential philosophers are alleged by him to have in common—which is that the only way to answer the ontological question is to attend to that 'immediate experience' in which 'being' discloses itself.

[19] *Ibid.*, p. 22.

The Conditions of Experience

awareness of the 'subject-object' (or 'self-world') structure—within which it is impossible to distinguish between the 'subject' of the experience and the 'object' experienced. (i) would be required by the thesis that the 'self-world structure' is what makes experience *as such* possible. (ii) would be required by the claim that it is in 'immediate experience' that the basic ontological structure is disclosed—where 'immediate experience' is characterisable (negatively) as the sort of experience to which the 'subject-object' (or 'self-world') distinction of Tillich's basic ontological doctrine is inapplicable.

This last criticism is decisive from the point of view of the attempt to determine whether Tillich succeeds in rendering plausible the contention that the question about what makes experience possible (on the second interpretation) is an *ontological* question. For whatever be the fate of the claim that 'immediate experience' is the source of our knowledge of the basic ontological structure, it would appear that it cannot be this structure which makes experience possible since there is a kind of experience—viz. 'immediate experience'—which does not exhibit this structure. Tillich's question about the basic ontological structure thus cannot be identical with his question about the conditions of experience.

Chapter 5

ONTOLOGY AND THE VERB 'TO BE'

The ontological question is often formulated by Tillich as a question about the meaning of the verb 'to be'. I shall try to show, in this chapter and the next, how this formulation of the ontological question is linked in Tillich's mind both with the view that the ontologist's task is to *describe* the most general features of the things which 'are' and with the view that it is his task to *account for* the fact that there is a world at all. In both cases I shall try to formulate the assumptions, conscious and unconscious, which enable Tillich to further specify what appears to be a merely conceptual question in ways which make it intelligible, even if not defensible, for him to regard the question as calling for an ontological answer. It should be emphasised at the outset not only that Tillich does not consciously separate these two strands in his thought, but also that their confusion is rendered the easier by the fact that in the final outcome the ontologist must set about doing the same thing whether it is the descriptive or the explanatory ontological question that he takes himself to be tackling.

I shall begin by quoting at length some of the more important passages in which the first of these two strands in Tillich's thought about the ontological question is exhibited.

'The ontological question is What is being-itself? What is that which is not a special being or a group of beings, not something concrete or something abstract, but rather something which is always thought implicitly, and sometimes

Ontology and the Verb 'To Be'

explicitly, if something is said to *be*? Philosophy aks the question of being as being. It investigates the character of everything that is in so far as it is. This is its basic task ...'[1]
'Philosophy asks the ultimate question that can be asked, namely, the question as to what being, simply being, means. Whatever the object of thought may be, it is always something that *is* and not *not is*. But what does this word "is" mean? What is the meaning of being? ... What is the structure in which every being participates? ... [For] philosophy asks the question concerning being itself. This implies that philosophy primarily does not ask about the special character of the beings, the things and events, the ideas and values, the souls and bodies which share being. Philosophy asks what about this being itself ... [But] philosophy ... tries to understand being itself and the categories and structure which are common to all kinds of beings.'[2]
'What does it mean that something *is*? What are the characteristics of everything that participates in being? ... This is the question of ontology ... Ontology asks the simple and infinitely difficult question: What does it mean to *be*? What are the structures, common to everything that is, to everything that participates in being? One cannot avoid this question by denying that there are such common structures. One cannot deny that being is one and that the qualities and elements of being constitute a texture of connected and conflicting forces. This texture is one, in so far as it *is* ... It is one but it is neither a dead identity nor a repetitious sameness. It is one in the manifoldness of its texture. Ontology is the attempt to describe this texture ... Ontology characterises the texture of being itself, which is effective in everything that is ... And being is an infinitely involved texture, to be described by the never-ending task of ontology.'[3]

In all three passages the ontological question is identified as a

---
[1] Tillich, *Systematic Theology* (Vol. I), p. 181.
[2] Tillich, *The Protestant Era*, p. 86.
[3] Tillich, *Love, Power and Justice*, pp. 19-20.

Paul Tillich

question about the meaning of a certain expression and this question is said to require for its answer a description of the features shared by all 'kinds of beings'. I shall first identify a set of assumptions which facilitate the identification of this ostensibly conceptual question with the ontological question Tillich envisages. I shall then try to show that Tillich in fact makes these assumptions. Finally, after drawing attention to the dubiousness of some of these assumptions, I shall offer a partial explanation of Tillich's acceptance of them.

I ASSUMPTIONS FACILITATING IDENTIFICATION OF THE QUESTION ABOUT THE MEANING OF THE VERB 'TO BE' WITH THE ONTOLOGICAL QUESTION

1. Perhaps the major assumption which must be made if the elucidation of the meaning of the verb 'to be' [4] is to be identified with the description of the 'structures' common to all 'beings' is that the meaning of such words as 'is' and 'are' can be identified with some 'element' [5] in the real world. Clearly if the words 'is' and 'are' *mean* whatever they stand for or represent, then the obvious way to elucidate their meaning is to identify/describe what they stand for or represent; and if what they stand for or represent is some 'element' in the real world, then it is this 'element' which must be identified/described if their meaning is to be explained.

2. If the elucidation of the meaning of the words 'is' and 'are' is to involve not only the identification/description of some 'element' in the real world (cf. assumption 1) but, more specifically, the *description* of the features *common* to all the things to which these words can be applied, then it is presumably being

---

[4] It is the so-called 'existential' use of the verb 'to be' in which Tillich is interested in this context: I shall follow Tillich in ignoring the uses of the verb which are exemplified in such sentences as 'The evening star *is* the morning star' (the so-called 'is' of identity) and 'Socrates *is* mortal' (the so-called 'is' of predication).

[5] I use the word 'element' in order to *avoid* any commitment in regard to the ontological status of whatever the words 'is' and 'are' stand for: properties, relations, and particulars, for example, are all 'elements' in the sense intended here.

taken for granted that 'is' and 'are' function as descriptive words in the sentences in which they occur.

3. If the characteristics to be described in the course of elucidation of the meaning of the words 'is' and 'are' are to be characteristics shared by *everything that is*', then it must be possible to apply these words to all the things in the world.

4. If the characteristics to be described by the ontologist are to be characteristics *common* to all the things in the world, then the words 'is' and 'are' must be univocal: unless the words 'is' and 'are' mean the same thing on all occasions of their use, then even if they are descriptive expressions (cf. assumption 2) and even if there is nothing to which they may not be applied (cf. assumption 3), the characteristics for which they stand will not be characteristics *common* to all the things to which they apply.

To sum up: the question Tillich asks about the meaning of the verb 'to be' will be identical with the question about the characteristics common to absolutely all the things in the world, if (1) the meaning of the words 'is' and 'are' can be identified with some 'element' in the real world, (2) this element is some characteristic of particular things in the real world, (3) this characteristic is *common* to all the things to which the words 'is' and 'are' can be applied, and (4) the words 'is' and 'are' may be applied to *all* the 'things' in the world.[6]

II DOES TILLICH ACCEPT THESE ASSUMPTIONS?

It might be thought that Tillich's subscription to these assumptions could be inferred from the fact that they facilitate the identification of the question about the meaning of the verb 'to be' with the question about the 'structures common to everything that is'—when this is considered in conjunction with the fact (documented above) that Tillich does effect this identification. But this would be a mistake. For these assumptions, while

---

[6] In this summary, it should be noted, the third and fourth assumptions stated earlier appear as (4) and (3) respectively. I shall continue to refer to them in the discussion which follows as the third and fourth assumptions, however.

Paul Tillich

jointly sufficient to enable Tillich to convert his ostensibly conceptual question into an overtly ontological one, are not, as a set, necessary for this purpose. Indeed it is an important part of the argument of the next chapter that Tillich contrives to effect the identification of these questions in quite a different way *also*.

Since Tillich nowhere betrays any awareness of the *prima facie* oddness of his formulation of the question about the meaning of the verb 'to be' as a question about the characteristics shared by all the things in the world, he nowhere articulates the assumptions which make it possible for the question to be formulated in this way. *A fortiori* he nowhere attempts to defend these assumptions. The evidence that Tillich does in fact subscribe to these assumptions is for the most part indirect and in consequence perhaps less than conclusive.

Take the first assumption. Does Tillich assume that the words 'is' and 'are' mean what they stand for or represent, where what they stand for or represent is some 'element' in the real world? It is not possible to cite in support of an affirmative answer any passage in which just this question is discussed by Tillich. But the absence of direct evidence of this sort is neither surprising nor fatal to the claim that he does make some such assumption. It is not surprising because only a philosopher who is aware of the diversity of the functions performed by words is likely to preface a discussion of the meaning of the words 'is' and 'are' with an investigation of the question whether they have meaning in virtue of the fact that they stand for or point to or represent something or whether they have meaning in virtue of the fact that they perform some other function in discourse.[7] And although, as will be seen, Tillich does distinguish between the 'denotative' and the 'expressive' functions of language, the fact that he thinks that these two functions between them exhaust the possibilities, when taken in conjunction with the fact that 'is'

---

[7] Even so language-conscious a philosopher as G. E. Moore found it natural to identify the question 'What does the word "good" *mean*?' with the question 'What does the word "good" stand for?' and did not so much as consider whether this identification might be questionable enough to call for defence (cf. *Principia Ethica*, Chapter 1).

Ontology and the Verb 'To Be'

and 'are' obviously do not perform an 'expressive' function, makes it understandable that Tillich should not consider it necessary to raise the question whether 'is' and 'are' have meaning in virtue of the fact they they stand for or represent something. Nor is Tillich's failure to consider this question fatal to the claim that he does in fact assume that 'is' and 'are' stand for or represent some 'element' of the real world. For such occasional remarks [8] as he does make about the nature of language in general suggest that he regards all words with the possible exception of words which serve an expressive function as having meaning in virtue of what they stand for or represent.

Consider, for example, the passage in which Tillich distinguishes between the 'expressive' and the 'denotative' functions of language.

> 'The word communicates the self-related and unapproachable experience of an ego-self to another in two ways: by expression and by denotation . . . The denotative power of language is its ability to grasp and communicate general meanings. The expressive power of language is its ability to disclose and to communicate personal states.' [9]

The distinction is stated so obscurely that there is some justification for the complaint that Tillich is not here distinguishing between two *functions* of language at all. There is no clear rejection of the view that both words which 'express' and words which 'denote' stand for or represent what they 'express' or 'denote': it seems possible that Tillich is grounding the distinction between 'expression' and 'denotation', not in any difference he detects between 'standing for' as a mode of 'having meaning' and some other mode, but in a difference he detects between two sorts of thing for which words may stand. Thus he might be taken to be claiming that when words stand for 'meanings' which are publicly accessible they must be said to 'denote' what they stand for, but

---

[8] These remarks are certainly very far from providing, even in germ, a philosophy of language; they must, however, serve here as evidence since Tillich nowhere sets out a philosophy of language.

[9] *Systematic Theology* (Vol. I), p. 137.

Paul Tillich

that when what they stand for are 'personal states' (and therefore *not* publicly accessible) they must be said to 'express' what they stand for. If this interpretation of the distinction were sound, then the existence of a distinction in Tillich between 'expression' and 'denotation' would not be evidence against, but rather evidence in favour of, the hypothesis that he assumes that *all* words have meaning in virtue of the fact that they stand for something.

But even if Tillich should have to be interpreted as holding that words which denote perform a different function from words which express, the distinction is not fatal to the claim that Tillich assumes that 'is' and 'are' function denotatively. For while it would be ideal to be able to bolster this claim by confirming the hypothesis that for Tillich *all* words (and therefore, *a fortiori*, the words 'is' and 'are') have meaning in virtue of the fact that they stand for or represent something, it is possible to support the claim just as effectively by appealing to the fact that for Tillich all words, with the exception of those which perform an 'expressive' function, have meaning in virtue of the fact that they stand for or represent something—*if* it can be shown that 'is' and 'are' do not perform an 'expressive' function. And it is difficult to imagine any interpretation of 'expressive' in the passage cited which would for a moment lend support to the contention that 'is' and 'are' are thought by Tillich to perform an 'expressive' function.[10]

The second, third and fourth assumptions may be considered together. Once the vital link between questions about the meanings of words and questions about the nature of reality provided by acceptance of the first assumption has been established, it is easy to show that for Tillich the 'element' in the real world which constitutes the meaning of the words 'is' and 'are' is a *characteristic*—or structure, or feature—*common* to *all* the things in the world. (Assumption 2 emphasises that the 'element' in the real world for which 'is' and 'are' stand is a characteristic or general feature and not—as it might well be for

---

[10] Especially since later in the passage, Tillich gives an 'outcry' as an example of an 'almost exclusively expressive' use of language. See *Systematic Theology* (Vol. I), p. 137.

all that acceptance of assumption 1 involves to the contrary—a particular or individual. Assumption 3 emphasises that this 'element' is detectable in *all* the things in the world. Assumption 4 stresses that it is indeed *one and the same* element which is discoverable in all the things in the world.) That Tillich subscribes to these assumptions can be shown by drawing attention to relevant parts of the passages quoted at the beginning of this chapter. 'Philosophy ... tries to understand being itself and the categories and structures which are *common* to *all* kinds of beings.' [11] 'What does it mean that something *is*? What are the *characteristics* of *everything* that participates in being? ... What does it mean to *be*? What are the structures, *common* to *everything* that is, to *everything* that participates in being.' [12] The second of these passages is particularly interesting because of the close juxtaposition of the question about the meaning of the verb 'to be' and the question about the characteristics common to all the things that there are: the latter is so obviously intended as an elucidatory reformulation of the former that it is impossible not to conclude that for Tillich the words 'is' and 'are' stand for 'characteristics common to everything that participates in being'.

III DISCUSSION OF ASSUMPTIONS

In discussing the assumptions underlying Tillich's ontological formulation of the question about the verb 'to be', I shall be as concerned to account for his implicit acceptance of these assumptions as to argue that some of them are false.

Tillich is clearly impressed by what he takes to be the fact that there is nothing to which the words 'is' and 'are' may not be applied.[13] Now it would be one thing to hold that no *a priori* limit can be set to the possible values of 'x' in such sentences as 'There is such a thing as x' where 'x' is a substantival expression

[11] *The Protestant Era*, p. 86 (my italics).
[12] *Love, Power and Justice*, p. 19 ('is' and 'be' are italicised by Tillich; otherwise italics mine).
[13] Assumption 3.

of some sort. But when Tillich takes it for granted that 'is' and 'are' may be applied to *all* the things in the world, he seems to be assuming that the words 'is' and 'are' are the grammatical predicates of the sentences in which they occur. This is clear, I think, from his penchant for formulating the question about the meaning of the verb 'to be' in the words: 'What does it mean that something *is*?' [14] The truth is, however, that the words 'is' and 'are' are *never* usable as predicate-expressions. There are no values of '*x*' which would enable one to say '*x is*'.

Tillich might try to escape this criticism by claiming that he is concerned to discover the *true* meaning of the verb 'to be' through investigation of the most fundamental features of the world and can consequently afford to be indifferent to the way in which this verb is ordinarily used. It is worth asking, however, whether there is any reason to suppose that the real meaning of the verb 'to be' (if we do not cavil at the assumption that there is such a thing) is more likely to be ascertained if 'is' and 'are' are represented as the grammatical predicates of the sentences in which they occur—when this is one way in which these words are *never* ordinarily used.[15]

This question becomes urgent when two of the risks inherent in such a procedure are identified. In the first place, there is the danger that the morphological resemblance between such factitious 'is'- and 'are'-sentences and other predicative sentences will have some effect on the way in which the question about the meaning of the words 'is' and 'are' is further specified and consequently on the way in which an answer to this question is sought. It is difficult to believe that this is a danger Tillich has

---

[14] See *Love, Power and Justice*, p. 19; *Biblical Religion and the Search for Ultimate Reality*, p. 6; *The Protestant Era*, p. 85.

[15] It may be possible to account, in part, for the fact that Tillich represents 'is' and 'are' as grammatically predicative expressions when formulating the ontological problem by reference to the fact that the verbs 'to be' and 'to exist' mean much the same thing in some contexts, when this is taken in conjunction with the fact that 'exists' *can* occur as the grammatical predicate of sentences in which it is used. But even if this should be part of what explains Tillich's assumption that 'is' and 'are' can be represented as the grammatical predicates of the sentences in which they occur, it can hardly be regarded as part of the justification.

Ontology and the Verb 'To Be'

escaped: is there, for example, no connection between his assumption that 'is' and 'are' are grammatically predicative expressions and his tendency to assume that they function descriptively? In the second place, for the use of 'is' which Tillich is investigating to be *toto caelo* different from its ordinary use(s) makes it virtually inevitable that it should be a 'context-free' use: and this strengthens Tillich's tendency to suppose that the meanings of such words as 'is' and 'are' can be ascertained through exclusive attention to what they are used to 'point to', and *a fortiori* without attention to the conditions under which or the contexts in which they may be used.

Although the assumption that 'is' and 'are' occur univocally in all the sentences in which they occur is an assumption which Tillich nowhere investigates—and any investigation he might have undertaken would, in any case, have been seriously handicapped by his concentration upon factitious 'is'- and 'are'-sentences in which 'is' and 'are' occur as the grammatical predicates and by his resultant indifference to the variety of contexts in which the more authentic 'is'- and 'are'-sentences in ordinary use are used—it is not true that Tillich offers nothing in the way of defence of this assumption. In an attempt to come to terms with a possible objection to his contention that the way to ascertain the meaning of the words 'is' and 'are' is to find out what is *common* to all the things to which these words can be applied—viz. the objection that perhaps there is nothing common to all these things—Tillich writes: 'One cannot deny that being is one and that the qualities and elements of being constitute a texture of connected and conflicting forces. This texture is one, in so far as it *is*. . . .' [16] Tillich's reply to this objection, in essence, is that there *must* be something common to all the things to which 'is' and 'are' may be applied, precisely because a single word ('is' or 'are') is applicable to all of them. The presupposition—that our ability to say of all these things that they 'are' would be unintelligible if they did not have something in

[16] *Love, Power and Justice*, p. 19.

Paul Tillich

common—is, of course, false [17] and Tillich's reply in consequence unsatisfactory. Despite its unsatisfactoriness, it is of interest as accounting in part for his acceptance of the assumption that 'is' and 'are' occur univocally in the sentences in which they occur.[18]

That the verb 'to be' does not perform a descriptive function has been too often demonstrated to be argued here. The interesting question is why Tillich should so often have written as though it did.[19] Two reasons are worth considering. The first is that a philosopher who is simultaneously committed to a denotative theory of meaning and convinced that the words 'is' and 'are' are applicable to all the things in the world is almost bound to suppose that the 'something' for which these words stand is some general feature of the things to which they can be applied: and that is tantamount to supposing that 'is' and 'are' are descriptive words. The second is the temptation inherent in Tillich's view that 'is' and 'are' are the grammatical predicates of the sentences in which they occur, the temptation of being seduced by the structural similarity between 'is'- and 'are'-sentences (as Tillich represents them) and other grammatically predicative sentences into supposing that 'is' and 'are' function in just the

---

[17] Cf. J. L. Austin's attack on this presupposition in his paper 'The Meaning of a Word' (included in *'Philosophy and Ordinary Language* edited by Charles E. Caton). Austin's thesis in the third section of the paper is that *'it is not in the least true* that all the things which I "call by the same (general) name" *are* in general "similar", in any ordinary sense of that much abused word' (p. 15).

[18] One recent attempt to differentiate the (allegedly) different uses of 'is'- and 'are'-sentences—that is, of sentences of the form 'There is . . .' and 'There are . . .' —is to be found in Kurt Baier's paper on 'Existence' (*Proceedings of the Aristotelian Society*, 1960-1).

[19] I hestitate to say outright that Tillich assumes that 'is' and 'are' are descriptive words, despite the fact that the passages quoted at the beginning of this chapter contain statements which seem to be intelligible on no other basis, because there is some evidence that Tillich, despite his final identification of the question about the meaning of the verb 'to be' with the question about the structure common to all kinds of beings, was endeavouring to make sense of what he couldn't but half-recognise to be the non-descriptive force of 'is'- and 'are'-statements. This evidence will be reviewed in the next chapter, where it will be shown that alongside the view that the question about the meaning of the verb 'to be' is identifiable straightforwardly with the question about the structures common to everything that is (the view at present under discussion) there is to be found the view that this question is to be identified with the question about what enables what 'is' to 'be' and not 'not be', confronted as all beings are by the 'threat of non-being'.

Ontology and the Verb 'To Be'

way in which the grammatical predicates of other grammatically predicative sentences function. Doubtless Tillich is mistaken if he supposes that all grammatically predicative sentences other than his own 'is'- and 'are'-sentences have descriptive terms as their predicates, but the fact remains that many have and some at any rate of the rest are thought by Tillich to.[20]

The denotative theory of meaning [21] is false both because 'standing for' is not the only function fulfilled by words and because even of those words which are used to stand for something it is incorrect to hold that their meaning is identical with what they stand for. Although Tillich may be prepared to grant that some words serve an 'expressive' function (and as has been noted it is not at all clear how Tillich's distinction between 'expression' and 'denotation' ought to be interpreted: not at all clear, in particular, whether the distinction is one between two different functions of words at all), this concession, by its very meagreness, fails to throw any light on the use of 'is' and 'are', since these words do not fulfil an 'expressive' function. It might have been as obvious to Tillich that these words do not function *denotatively* had he considered such (unproblematic) uses of 'is' as 'There *is* such a place as Edinburgh' instead of such (problematic) uses as 'Edinburgh *is*'. 'Uses' like the latter seem to suggest a way of adhering to the denotative theory for such a word as 'is' precisely because they suggest the possibility of construing 'is' as a descriptive word—i.e. as a word which denotes or stands for a *characteristic*. There is, by contrast, no way of making sense of 'is' as it is used in sentences of the (more authentic) 'There is such a place as Edinburgh' type under the auspices of the denotative theory.

[20] Evaluative sentences, e.g. are often grammatically predicative sentences, as in 'Pleasure is good', yet Tillich is of the opinion that such sentences must be taken to be descriptive: the major problem of ethics is in his view the problem of showing how value-words can be regarded as standing for certain fundamental features of reality.
[21] Cf. Assumption 1.

Chapter 6

THE MYSTERY OF BEING

Although, as has been noted in the last chapter, Tillich seems sometimes to assume that 'is' and 'are' are descriptive words—it is this assumption chiefly which enables him to identify the question concerning the meaning of the verb 'to be' with the question concerning the 'structures' which are common to 'everything that is'—there are passages in his writings which betray his uneasiness about this assumption. In the Introduction to the second volume of *Systematic Theology*,[1] for example, he inveighs against critics of his use of the concept of being in the first volume of this work for gratuitously attributing to him a use of this concept which he is anxious to repudiate. His critics have misunderstood his use of the concept of being, Tillich claims, because they have assumed that the 'concept of being represents the highest possible abstraction'. That is, they have taken 'being' to be the 'genus to which all other genera are subordinated with respect to universality and with respect to the degree of abstraction'. Tillich's answer to such critics is that 'the concept of being does not have the character that nominalism attributed to it. It is not the highest abstraction . . .' Rather it is the 'expression of the experience of being over against non-being. Therefore it can be described as the power of being which resists non-being'. And this conception of 'being' 'lies beyond the conflict of nominalism and realism'. 'The same word, the emptiest of all concepts when taken as an abstraction, becomes

[1] Tillich, *Systematic Theology* (Vol. II), pp. 11–12.

the most meaningful of all concepts when it is understood as the power of being in everything that has being.'

That Tillich, despite this emphatic denial, does frequently conceive of 'being' as the 'highest abstraction'—that is, as standing for what is common to absolutely *all* 'beings'—has already been argued at sufficient length. The denial, however, is of interest as pointing to an interpretation of 'the question of being' quite unlike that considered in the last chapter, albeit resembling it in that it too is designed by Tillich to throw light on the meaning of the verb 'to be', and also in that it too requires of the ontologist a scrutiny of the structures common to 'everything that is'.

I want in this chapter to consider how Tillich contrives to link up his interest in the question about the meaning of the verb 'to be' with his preoccupation with the ontological question in a form which seems not to presuppose that the concept of being is 'the highest abstraction'.

I   THE VERB 'TO BE' AND THE STRUCTURES
    COMMON TO ALL BEINGS: ANOTHER VIEW

How, then, does Tillich manage to identify the question about the meaning of the verb 'to be' with the question about the 'structures' common to all beings *without* assuming that 'is' and 'are' are descriptive terms designating some feature common to all beings?

The identification is effected in two stages, I suggest. First, it is assumed that to know the meaning of 'is' and 'are' statements is to know what enables us to *say* of the things which 'are' *that they 'are'*—and it is not noticed that there is no need to identify what enables *us* to *say* of the things which 'are' that they 'are' with what enables *these things themselves* 'to be'. Second, the question 'What is it that enables the things which are *to be*?' is identified—for reasons which will be investigated below—with the question 'What are the structures common to all beings?'

Paul Tillich

There is no *direct* evidence in Tillich's writings of a tendency to confuse the question 'What enables us to say of the things which are that they are?' with the question 'What is it that enables the things which are *to be*?' However, if it can be assumed that Tillich would take for granted the existence of a close connection between our understanding of sentences embodying finite parts of the verb 'to be' and our knowledge of what enables us to *say* of the things which 'are' *that* they 'are', and if it can be established that Tillich does eventually identify the question 'What is it which enables the things which are *to be*?' with the question 'What are the structures common to all beings?', then the fact that Tillich does suppose that light is thrown on the question of the meaning of the verb 'to be' by his answer to the question 'What is it that enables what is "to be"?' will perhaps serve as reasonably satisfactory *indirect* evidence of a tendency on Tillich's part to confuse these questions. I shall focus attention in the rest of this chapter, consequently, on the reasons which underlie Tillich's eventual identification of the question 'What is it that enables what is *to be*?' with the question 'What are the structures common to all the things which *are*?'

To see how this identification is effected, it is necessary to explore that strand in Tillich's thought according to which the ontological question springs from what he calls 'the shock of possible nonbeing'.

> 'The ontological question, the question of being-itself, arises in something like a "metaphysical shock"—the shock of possible nonbeing.' [2]
>
> 'The threat of nonbeing, grasping the mind, produces "the ontological shock" ... "Shock" points to a state of mind in which the mind is thrown out of its normal balance, shaken in its structure ... This experience of ontological shock is expressed in the cognitive function by the basic philosophical question, the question of being and nonbeing.' [3]

[2] *Ibid.* (Vol. I), p. 181.
[3] *Ibid.* (Vol. I), p. 126.

11 THE SHOCK OF NONBEING AND THE MYSTERY OF BEING

The 'shock of nonbeing' [4] is occasioned, according to Tillich, by recognition of the 'mystery of being'—where the 'mystery of being' consists in the fact 'that there is something and not nothing'. Consider the following passages:

> 'The question of being is produced by the "shock of nonbeing". Only man can ask the ontological question because he alone is able to look beyond the limits of his own being and of every other being. Looked at from the standpoint of possible nonbeing, being is a mystery. Man is free to take this standpoint because he is free to transcend every given reality. He is not bound to "beingness"; he can envisage nothingness; he can ask the ontological question.' [5]
>
> 'The genuine mystery appears when reason is driven beyond itself ... to the fact that "being is and nonbeing is not" (Parmenides), to the original fact that there is *something* and not *nothing*.' [6]
>
> 'The question of being ... is the question of what it means to *be*. It is the simplest, most profound, and absolutely inexhaustible question—the question of what it means to say that something *is*. This word "is" hides the riddle of all riddles, the mystery that there is anything at all.[7] Every philosophy whether it asks the question of being openly or not, moves around this mystery, has a partial answer to it, whether acknowledged or not, but is generally at a loss to answer it fully.' [8]

Now if it is the recognition of the 'mystery of being'—where

---

[4] Tillich also refers to the 'shock of nonbeing' as the 'ontological shock' and as the 'metaphysical shock'—presumably because he thinks it gives rise to the ontological (or metaphysical) question.

[5] *Systematic Theology* (Vol. I), p. 207.

[6] *Ibid.*, p. 122.

[7] Notice the connection this passage establishes between the question about the meaning of the verb 'to be' and the sort of ontological question which is generated by the 'metaphysical shock'—i.e. by recognition of the 'mystery of being', the mystery 'that there is anything at all'.

[8] Tillich, *Biblical Religion and the Search for Ultimate Reality*, p. 6.

Paul Tillich

this is constituted by the fact that there is something and not nothing—which occasions the 'shock of nonbeing', the experience of this shock must not be confused with the experience of 'anxiety' (defined as 'the existential awareness of non-being'). It is one thing for a man to be aware that he will die some day and quite another for him to be struck by the mysteriousness of the fact that there is a world at all. The two are not even necessarily connected. For, on the one hand, it is surely conceivable that a man should experience 'anxiety' on those occasions on which he faces up to the fact that he is mortal without, on those occasions (or perhaps ever), being afflicted by a sense of the mysteriousness of the fact 'that there is something and not nothing'. On the other hand, it is not inconceivable that a man who is convinced of his own immortality should nevertheless be struck by the mysteriousness of the fact that there is a world at all.[9]

Although these experiences are clearly different, however, the language Tillich uses in describing them facilitates their confusion, thereby contributing to the assimilation of the quite different questions they respectively generate. In one place,[10] for example, Tillich claims that it is the 'threat of non-being' which 'produces the "ontological shock"' and can write consequently of 'the "shock" which grasps the mind when it encounters the threat of nonbeing'. Yet it is precisely the 'threat of nonbeing' which is said to give rise to 'anxiety'.[11] Since, as has already been noted,[12] Tillich sometimes grounds the impulse to philosophise in the experience of 'anxiety', it is not surprising that there is no recognition on his part of the difference between the sort of question which is generated in this way and the sort of question

---

[9] This seems to be the sort of thing Wittgenstein hints at darkly (*Tractatus Logico-Philosophicus* 6.4312) when he says: 'Not only is there no guarantee of the temporal immortality of the human soul, that is to say of its eternal survival after death; but, in any case, this assumption completely fails to accomplish the purpose for which it has always been intended. Or is some riddle solved by my surviving for ever? Is not this eternal life itself as much of a riddle as our present life?'

[10] *Systematic Theology* (Vol. I), p. 126.

[11] Tillich, *The Courage To Be*, p. 41. This view was discussed in Chapter 1.

[12] Cf. *Biblical Religion and the Search for Ultimate Reality*, p. 6.

The Mystery of Being

which is allegedly occasioned by awareness of the 'mystery of being'.

But what sort of experience is the experience of the 'mystery of being'? [13] What is there about the fact that the world exists ('that there is something and not nothing') which enables Tillich to claim that to recognise this fact is to stand in the presence of a 'mystery'?

There are at least two incompatible ways in which Tillich conceives of the 'mystery of being'. To bring out the difference between them, it will be useful to contrast three attitudes which might conceivably be adopted towards the fact that the world exists. In the first place, it is possible to believe in the contingency of the fact that there is a world at all while denying that this fact either requires, or admits of, explanation. *That* the world exists is, from this point of view, a 'brute' fact, a fact which simply has to be accepted. Secondly, it might be argued that it is not only undesirable to regard the existence of the world as a brute fact to be accepted despite its 'opacity' to our understanding, but also unnecessary, since the world can be shown to be a thoroughly rational system. When the world is viewed from this vantage-point, it would be claimed, its existence ceases to be a 'brute' fact and becomes a thoroughly intelligible, 'luminous' fact. Thirdly, it might be held that the existence of the world requires to be explained all right but that the required explanation is one which necessarily eludes the grasp of our intellects. The existence of the world is, for the advocate of this third view, a 'mysterious' fact: it is neither (as on the first view) a merely unproblematic fact which simply has to be accepted, nor (as on the second view) a sheerly intelligible fact. The existence of the world is a problematic fact, but the problem it poses is not susceptible of any solution. An explanation of the existence of the world seems to be required and yet none seems to be available.

---

[13] An interesting discussion of this experience is to be found in Wittgenstein's 'Lecture on Ethics' (published posthumously in *The Philosophical Review*, Vol. CXXIV, No. 1, pp. 3–12). 'I believe the best way of describing (this experience) is to say that when I have it I *wonder at the existence of the world*. And I am then inclined to use such phrases as "how extraordinary that anything should exist" or "how extraordinary that the world should exist".' (p. 8).

Paul Tillich

It is between the second and the third of these views that Tillich seems to oscillate. The second view seems to be required by the claim that the 'shock of nonbeing' (which is occasioned, of course, as has been seen, precisely by recognition of the fact 'that there is something and not nothing') generates the question which it is the philosopher's (or more accurately, the ontologist's) central task to try to answer: for the third view expressly rules out the possibility of any answer being returned to the question generated by the 'shock of nonbeing'. Yet the third view (or something like it) seems to be required by Tillich's deployment of the key-term 'mystery' (in 'mystery of being') in an avowedly technical sense, one which precludes the possibility of any rational exploration of the 'mysterious'.

The view that no cognitive approach (and *a fortiori* no philosophical approach) to the 'mystery of being' is possible is clearly stated in the passage [14] in which it is alleged that 'the fact that "being is and non-being is not"', that 'there is something and not nothing', is a 'mystery'. In this passage Tillich emphasises that he is using the word 'mystery' in a special technical sense. He warns:

> 'In order to safeguard the proper use of the word "mystery", uses which are wrong or confusing must be avoided. "Mystery" should not be applied to something which ceases to be a mystery after it has been revealed. Nothing which can be discovered by a methodical cognitive approach should be called a "mystery". What is not known today, but which might possibly be known tomorrow, is not a mystery'.

Although there is here a hint—which is developed, to some extent, in a subsequent passage [15]—that there can be disclosure of the 'mysterious' in 'revelation' (though not, even so, the sort of disclosure which removes the 'mysteriousness' of what has been 'revealed'), Tillich's remarks seem unambiguously to rule out the possibility of any rational exploration of the 'mysterious'.

[14] *Systematic Theology* (Vol. I), pp. 121–2.
[15] *Ibid.*, p. 123.

The Mystery of Being

Since Tillich certainly conceives of philosophy (or ontology) as a *rational* discipline, this is tantamount to an admission that the philosopher as such can make no contribution (through the answering of the ontological question generated by the 'shock of nonbeing') to the disclosure of the 'mystery of being'.

III THE MYSTERY OF BEING AND
     THE ONTOLOGICAL QUESTION

Turning to the other of the views concerning the 'mystery of being' to which Tillich subscribes intermittently—namely, the view that experience of the 'shock of nonbeing' gives rise to the ontological question—it must be noted at the outset that no consistent view of the correct formulation of this question is adopted by Tillich. There are places in his writings in which he endorses without any qualms the 'Why is there something and not nothing?' formulation of the ontological question; and there are places in which he not only rejects this formulation as 'meaningless' but moves towards an identification of the question generated by the 'shock of nonbeing' with the question about the 'structures common to everything that has being'. I propose now to consider some of these passages with a view to discovering both why Tillich is alternately satisfied and dissatisfied with the 'Why is there something, why not nothing?' formulation and how he is able to move towards an identification of the question generated by the 'shock of nonbeing' with the very question which (as was shown in the last chapter) seems to presuppose that 'being' is a very general descriptive predicate.

I begin by quoting representative passages in which Tillich's varying attitudes towards the 'Why is there something, why not nothing?' formulation are expressed.

First, a couple of passages in which this formulation appears to receive Tillich's blessing. In his Union Theological Seminary inaugural lecture on 'Philosophy and Theology', Tillich links the question 'Why is there being and not not-being?' with what he claims is the central philosophical question, viz. 'What is the

Paul Tillich

meaning of being?' without betraying any anxiety in regard to its legitimacy.

> 'Philosophy asks the ultimate question that can be asked, namely, the question as to what being, simply being, means. Whatever the object of thought may be, it is always something that *is* and not *not is*. But what does the word "is" mean? What is the meaning of being? ... [The] experience out of which philosophy is born ... is the philosophical shock, the tremendous impetus of the questions: What is the meaning of being? Why is there being and not *not-being*? What is the structure in which every being participates?' [16]

Again, writing many years later, Tillich maintains that 'he who seriously asks the question, "Why is there something, why not nothing?" has experienced the shock of nonbeing', and there is no indication that seriously to entertain this question is to be taken in by an illegitimate question.[17]

Next, a couple of passages in which this formulation of the ontological question is called into question.

> (a) 'The ontological question, the question of being-itself arises in something like a metaphysical shock, the shock of possible non-being. This shock has been expressed in the question "Why is there something, why not nothing?" But in this form the question is meaningless, for every possible answer would be subject to the same question in an infinite regression. Thought must start with being; it cannot go behind it, as the form of the question itself shows. If one asks why there *is* not nothing, one attributes being even to nothing. Thought is based on being and it cannot leave this basis; but thought can imagine the negation of everything that *is*, and it can describe the nature and structure of being which give everything that is the power of resisting nonbeing.' [18]

---

[16] Tillich, *The Protestant Era*, p. 85.
[17] *Biblical Religion and the Search for Ultimate Reality*, p. 49.
[18] *Systematic Theology* (Vol. I), p. 182.

(b) 'It is, of course, misleading if one asks with some philosophers: "Why is there something? Why not nothing?" For this form of the question points to something that precedes being, from which being can be derived. But being can only be derived from being.' [19]

Prima facie, the formulation of the ontological question favoured by Tillich in the first couple of passages quoted above—viz. the question 'Why is there something, why not nothing?'—has the advantage of seeming to arise naturally out of the experience of 'the shock of nonbeing'. For it is natural to expect any question generated by awareness of the 'mystery of being' to be one the answer to which will tend to diminish our sense of the mysteriousness of the fact that there is a world. Now something of the mystery surrounding the very existence of the world would indeed be dissipated if anything could be said to render intelligible the fact that there *is* a world, in face of the fact that there *might* have been no world at all—if, in short, some *explanation* of the existence of the world could be provided. Since it appears to be the function of the question 'Why is there something, and not nothing?' to demand just such an explanation, it is *this* question, one is tempted to suppose, which must be thought by Tillich to be generated by experience of the 'shock of nonbeing'.

Why, then, does Tillich (in the second pair of passages quoted) profess to find difficulties in this formulation of the ontological question?

To ask 'Why is there something and not nothing?' is to ask why there is a world at all (where the 'world' comprises what*ever* 'is', *every*thing that 'is' [20]). But to ask 'Why is there a world at all?' is illegitimate (according to Tillich) because, and in so far as, it is to seek an explanation of the 'being' of 'everything that is' in terms of something other than 'what is'. Since there is, *ex hypothesi*, *nothing* over and above 'what is' to serve as a

[19] *Ibid.*, p. 126.
[20] 'Something', in Tillich's question, does *not* mean—as it normally does—some particular thing the identity of which is not clear.

Paul Tillich

referent in this explanation and since Tillich dismisses the suggestion that 'nonbeing' might account for, or explain, the 'being' of 'everything that is', he not surprisingly regards the demand for such an explanation as illegitimate. This, I assume, is the general import of (a) and (b) (quoted above). Thus, in (a), Tillich supports his rejection as 'meaningless' of the question 'Why is there something, why not nothing?' by claiming that 'thought must start with being; it cannot go behind it, as the form of the question itself shows. If one asks why there *is* not nothing, one attributes being even to nothing. Thought is based on being and it cannot leave this basis.' Taking for granted that the question 'Why is there something, why not nothing?' embodies a demand for the explanation of 'what is' in terms of 'what is not', Tillich denies that any such explanation is available: and the reason for its unavailability is simply the impossibility of 'thought' about 'nonbeing'. (If, *per impossibile*, the attempt to think about 'nonbeing' is made, 'nonbeing' is inevitably endowed with ontological standing.[21]) In (b), Tillich makes explicit the assumption that the form of the question 'Why is there something? Why not nothing?' requires that any answer to it be an attempt to derive 'what is' from something other than 'what is' (i.e. from 'what is not'): 'this form of the question points to something which precedes being, from which being can be derived.' He then has only to assert that the required derivation is impossible—'being can only be derived from being'—to be in a position to conclude that the question in this form is unsatisfactory.

Thus it is assumed in both passages—though the assumption is explicitly stated only in (b)—that a condition of the legitimacy of the 'Why is there something, why not nothing?' formulation of the ontological question is the possibility of 'derivation' of 'what is' from 'what is not', of 'being' from 'nonbeing'. In both passages, again, the question in this form is held to be illegitimate

---

[21] Elsewhere in his writings, as has been noted in Chapter 1, Tillich seems not at all opposed either to the view that we can conceive of 'nonbeing' or to the view that 'nonbeing' stands for a 'quality of being'.

The Mystery of Being

(in (a) it is said to be 'meaningless', in (b) to be 'misleading') precisely because the 'derivation' of 'what is' from 'what is not' is held to be impossible. In (b) it is simply asserted—as though it were self-evident—that 'being can only be derived from being'. In (a), by contrast, a reason is given in support of the claim that it is impossible for 'what is' to be derived from anything other than 'what is': the reason is that 'thought' cannot 'go behind' being, as it is 'based on being' and 'cannot leave this basis'. That from which 'what is' would have to be derived for any answer to the question 'Why is there something, why not nothing?' to be forthcoming is simply *unthinkable*; from which it follows that no such derivation is possible.

The passage from which (b) is taken affords no clue to the sort of formulation of the ontological question preferred by Tillich to the formulation (viz. 'Why is there something, why not nothing?') to which he objects. Indeed, at one point Tillich is in danger of giving the impression that no other formulation of the ontological question is available. When he claims that 'the meaning of this question can be expressed in the *statement* that being is the original fact which cannot be derived from anything else',[22] he seems to be closing the door to philosophical inquiry rather than opening it. In (a), by contrast, Tillich seems to want to move towards a reformulation of the question generated by the 'metaphysical shock', a reformulation which will take account of the main criticism directed against the question in its objectionable form, without jeopardising, however, the claim that experience of the 'shock of nonbeing' does indeed give rise to philosophical inquiry.

Unfortunately, no explicit reformulation of the ontological question is provided in (a). But from what is said explicitly about what 'thought' can do in coming to grips with the ontological question when it is properly formulated, it is not difficult to suggest a reformulation of the ontological question. (It should be recalled that in (a) it is what it is in principle impossible for 'thought' to do—viz. conceive of 'nonbeing'—which is represented

[22] *Systematic Theology* (Vol. I), p. 126.

Paul Tillich

as the ultimate reason for the impossibility of deriving 'what is' from 'what is not' in the manner assumed to be required by the 'Why is there something, why not nothing?' formulation of the ontological question.) Since 'thought ... can describe the nature and structure of being which give everything that is the power of resisting nonbeing' and since it is clear from the context that what 'thought' allegedly *can* do is bound up with the question of the possibility of an answer being returned to the question generated by the shock of nonbeing, the formulation of this question favoured by Tillich is presumably some such question as 'What is it which enables what *is* to *be?*' For if this be the ontological question, it is natural for him to say, in answer to it, that it is the 'nature and structure of being which give everything that is the power of resisting nonbeing'.[23]

But what, if anything, is gained by such a reformulation? The crucial difference between the sort of 'explanation' of the 'being' of 'everything that is' which Tillich rejects and the sort of 'explanation' he here seems prepared to welcome is that in the latter it is elements *within* the totality of 'what is' which are to be singled out as accounting for the 'being' of 'what is': it is the 'structure of being' (allegedly) which gives 'the power of resisting nonbeing' to 'everything that is', and this 'structure' is, of course, something which 'informs' all beings. It being in principle impossible to account for the 'being' of 'what is' by reference to something other than 'what is' (that is, by reference to 'what is not'), Tillich is prepared to look with favour on the suggestion that the desired explanation might be forthcoming if those 'elements' *within* the world which enable what 'is' to 'be' (to 'resist the threat of nonbeing') could be discriminated.

In effect, Tillich is rejecting the assumption which (on his view) underlies the 'Why is there something and not nothing?' formulation of the ontological question: the assumption that any explanation of the existence of the world must take the form of an attempt to 'derive' 'what is' from something other than 'what is'—in other words, from 'nonbeing'. That is, he is arguing (in

[23] *Ibid.*, p. 182.

effect) that there is no reason why the desired explanation should not take the form of a 'derivation' of 'what is' from selected 'elements' *within* the world—those elements which impart to whatever 'is' the ability (or the 'power', to use the word favoured by Tillich) to 'resist nonbeing'. In this way, the demand for an explanation of the existence of the world (which is precisely what is generated by experience of the 'shock of nonbeing') can be held to survive his demonstration of the impossibility of a certain sort of explanation.

Now there may, of course, be no such close connection as Tillich seems to take for granted between the formulation of the ontological question in the words 'Why is there something, why not nothing?' and the demand for the sort of explanation of the existence of the world which would involve the derivation of 'being' from 'nonbeing'. To ask the question 'Why is there something and not nothing?' (under the impact, let us suppose, of experience of the 'shock of nonbeing') may be simply to demand an explanation—*any* explanation—of the existence of the world which will contribute to the reduction of that sense of the mysteriousness of the fact that there is a world at all which is the source, after all, of the demand for explanation: there is no reason why it should be thought to be necessary *merely on account of the form of this question* for the explanation sought to consist in the derivation of 'what is' from 'what is not'. If this be the case, Tillich's rejection of the demand that 'what is' be shown to be derivable from 'what is not' is really a rejection, not of the question 'Why is there something and not nothing?' *as such*, but merely of the sort of demand this question is taken to embody, *on a certain interpretation of the question*.

If there is no such necessary connection as Tillich assumes there is between the form of the question 'Why is there something and not nothing?' and the demand that 'what is' be derived from 'what is not', and if his quarrel, in consequence, is really with the latter and not with the former, then some light is cast on the fact (illustrated above) that Tillich is by no means consistent in his denial that the question generated by the 'shock of nonbeing'

Paul Tillich

is the question 'Why is there something rather than nothing?' For if Tillich is really rejecting not this formulation of the question but rather the demand it embodies when interpreted in a certain way, then it is understandable that he should be inclined both to assert and to deny the meaninglessness of the question in this form. When his attention is directed towards that interpretation of this question which represents it as embodying the (in Tillich's view illegitimate) demand for a derivation of 'being' from 'nonbeing', he not surprisingly denies the meaningfulness of the question. But since it is not the question as such, but merely the demand it embodies when taken in a certain way which is illegitimate, it is natural that he should find it possible on occasion to formulate the question generated by the shock of nonbeing in the words 'Why is there something, why not nothing?'

We are now in a position to see how Tillich moves toward a formulation of the ontological question generated by the shock of nonbeing which is indistinguishable from that arrived at by the very different route traced in the last chapter. Confronted with a choice between abandoning altogether the demand for an explanation of the 'being' of 'what is' in face of his own demonstration of the illegitimacy of this demand on one straightforward interpretation of what it amounts to and attempting to reformulate this demand in a way which takes account of the main objection to the demand in its objectionable form, Tillich opts for the second of these alternatives. To account for the existence of the world by reference to something *outside* the world being in principle impossible, and to account for its existence in *some* way being nevertheless essential (the demand for some account being generated by the experience of the 'shock of nonbeing'), Tillich concludes that the sort of explanation sought by the ontologist must take the form of an explanation of the existence of the world in terms of those 'elements' or 'structures' *within* the world which enable the world to exist (which impart to 'what is' the 'power to resist nonbeing'). The description of these 'elements' or 'structures' thus becomes the task of the ontologist. Since the 'elements' or 'structures' which it is the

The Mystery of Being

ontologist's task to describe are assumed by Tillich to be the 'elements' or 'structures' *common* to all beings—presumably because all beings *alike* share in the 'power to resist nonbeing'—the question the ontologist bent upon diminishing our sense of the mysteriousness of the existence of the world finds himself committed to trying to answer is a question about what all beings have in common—which is just the question asked (for reasons considered in the last chapter) by the ontologist whose interest is in the meaning of the verb 'to be'.

IV ACCOUNTING FOR THE 'BEING' OF 'WHAT IS' AND DESCRIBING THE 'STRUCTURE' OF 'WHAT IS'

Hitherto, I have simply noted, without trying to make any sense of, the claim that the way to find out what enables existing things to exist is to try to ascertain the structure of these things. *Prima facie*, it is a peculiar claim to advance. It seems to be one thing to describe the nature of what is and quite another to account for the 'being' of what is. What is it that enables Tillich to advance this claim?

Part of the answer has already been supplied. That a description of the *nature* of what 'is' will also serve to explain *why* it 'is' is the sort of position suggested by the conjunction of two positions Tillich clearly wishes to adopt: (1) that some explanation of the existence of the world is required (cf. Tillich's thesis that the existence of the world is a mysterious fact which generates a philosophical problem), and (2) that any explanation which consists in attempting to derive the world from something other than the world is in principle impossible. For if there must needs be *some* explanation, and if the explanation cannot take the form of a derivation of the world from something other than the world, then the explanation must presumably take the form of identifying some element(s) *within* the world capable of accounting for the fact that there is a world.

But this sort of answer is clearly insufficient. For it does nothing to show what sort of connection there is between description of the structure of being and the sort of explanation sought by the ontologist. If the possibility of an explanation of the existence of the world hinges upon the possibility of identifying these *prima facie* different types of inquiry, then the absence of an intelligible account of the relation between these types of inquiry would be a reason for denying the possibility of any explanation of the existence of the world.

Can anything further be said to account for (even if not to justify) Tillich's tacit identification of two such disparate sorts of inquiry?

A link between accounting for (or explaining) the 'being' of 'what is' and describing the nature (or 'structure') of 'what is' can be provided if both of two views are attributed to Tillich. First, that the existence (or 'being') of particular things is traceable to their 'participation' in 'the power of being'; that it is the 'power of being' in everything that has being which accounts for the fact that these things 'are' at all. Second, that the 'power of being' in 'everything that it' expresses itself in, and manifests its presence through, the 'structure' or nature of 'what is'. If Tillich subscribes to both of these views, then it is understandable why he should confuse describing the 'structure' of 'what is' with explaining why 'what is' *is.*

Does Tillich, then, subscribe to these views? Take the first view—that particular 'beings' *are* in virtue of their 'participation' in the 'power of being'. Consider the following passages:

> (a) 'Ever since the time of Plato it has been known—although it has been disregarded, especially by the nominalists and their modern followers—that the concept of being as being, or being-itself, points to the power of being in everything, the power of resisting nonbeing.' [24]
>
> (b) 'Everything finite participates in being-itself... Otherwise it would not have the power of being. It would be swallowed by nonbeing, or it would never have emerged out of nonbeing.' [25]

[24] *Ibid.*, p. 261.
[25] *Ibid.*, p. 263.

The Mystery of Being

These passages make it clear that Tillich holds that all (finite) 'beings' 'participate in being-itself', where 'being-itself' is identical with 'the power of being in everything that is' [26] and that it is only in virtue of this 'participation in being-itself' (or in 'the power of being') that these things are able to 'emerge from nonbeing' and to 'resist the threat of nonbeing'. In short, it is only in virtue of their 'participation' in 'being-itself' or the 'power of being' that the things which 'are' are enabled to 'be'.

Textual evidence in support of the ascription to Tillich of the second view—the view that the 'power of being in everything that is' expresses itself in and through the 'structure' of 'what is' —is also easy to cite. Consider the following passages:

(a) '... the power of being ... expresses itself in and through the structure of being.' [27]

(b) 'Essence as that which makes a thing *what* it is ... empowers that which exists. It gives it its power of being.' [28]

(c) 'Thought ... can describe the nature and structure of being which give everything that is the power of resisting nonbeing.' [29]

Although these views of Tillich's help to account for his failure to distinguish between ontology *qua* endeavour to dispel something of the mystery of being and ontology *qua* endeavour to describe what all beings have in common, they are themselves in grave need of elucidation and defence. The claim that beings would not so much as 'be' were it not for their 'participation' in the 'power of being' seems to be intelligible only if it is taken to mean that the things which 'are' *are* only because they have the 'power to be'—i.e. because they have the *power* to exist, because they are *capable* of existing. Yet interpreted in this way, Tillich's claim lacks the explanatory force with which he clearly wants to see it invested. Moreover, if the 'power of being' in which all beings (allegedly) must 'participate' (in order to so much as 'be'

---

[26] These are explicitly identified in (a).
[27] *Systematic Theology* (Vol. I), p. 24.
[28] *Ibid.*, p. 225.
[29] *Ibid.*, p. 182.

Paul Tillich

at all) is 'ability or capacity to exist', Tillich's second view becomes sheerly unintelligible: for it makes no more sense to deny than it does to assert that the 'power of being' of a 'being' (in this sense of 'power of being') is identical with the properties it possesses.

To sum up. Although Tillich's characterisation of the fact that there is something and not nothing as a 'mystery' (in a special, technical sense of 'mystery') *ought* to make it impossible for him to claim that the shock of nonbeing administered by recognition of this fact is the source of a question which it is the ontologist's task to try to answer, Tillich does in fact claim that the ontological question is generated by the shock of nonbeing. This question is frequently formulated as the question 'Why is there something, why not nothing?', and Tillich's occasional attacks on the question in this form are, I think, best regarded as attacks on a certain plausible, but not strictly unavoidable, interpretation of this question. His rejection of this untenable interpretation of the question (his rejection, that is, of the demand for a 'derivation' of the world from something beyond, or outside, or other than, the world) does, however, have the effect of diminishing the difference between what the ontologist is committed to trying to do in grappling with the question 'Why is there something and not nothing?' and the ontological task described in the last chapter. For it transpires that to account for the fact that there is a world at all involves describing the 'structure of being' which gives to 'everything that is' the 'power to resist nonbeing'.

Chapter 7

THE CLARIFICATION OF CONCEPTS: I

In this chapter and the next I propose to consider the suggestion that there is a strand in Tillich's thought about the ontological question according to which it is the primary task of the ontologist to clarify concepts, that is, to try to get clear about the meanings of words. It has already been noted [1] that Tillich in places identifies the ontological question with the question about the meaning of the verb 'to be'; and two different ways in which this conceptual question has been 'ontologised' have been reviewed. The claim to be considered in this chapter, however, merits separate treatment despite its obvious affinity with the claim already considered, partly because the range of concepts calling for clarification, given the view here to be considered, is more extensive than that envisaged in the sort of ontological investigation discussed earlier, but also partly because this broader ontological programme is advocated for reasons which do not simply coincide with those already given. On the view to be considered in these chapters, for example, the clarification of the concepts of love, power and justice is no less an ontological task than the clarification of the concept of being; and these concepts are held to merit the attention of the ontologist for reasons which certainly do not reduce to (even if they should be regarded as including) such claims as that these concepts are applicable to 'everything that is' [2] or that elucidation of

[1] In Chapters 5 and 6.
[2] Cf. the claim in Chapter 5 that the concept of being applies to 'everything that is'.

Paul Tillich

these concepts will shed light on the 'mystery of being'. [3]

The view that it is the ontologist's task to undertake the clarification of concepts other than the concept of being—concepts, moreover, which (*prima facie*, at any rate) throw no light on the 'structure of being'—may conveniently be discussed with special reference to the argument of Tillich's *Love, Power and Justice*. For although Tillich maintains in this book that his central task is the clarification of the concepts of love, power and justice—that is, that the problem of the book concerns the meanings of the words 'love', 'power' and 'justice'—it is insisted that only the ontologist is equipped to carry out this task. Thus while Tillich acknowledges [4] that 'the help of the semanticist is perhaps in no realm so much needed as in the jungle of ambiguities which has grown up . . . in the sphere which is circumscribed by love, power and justice', yet it is not, in the event, the assistance of the 'semanticist' which is invoked: rather, it is to the 'ontologist' that Tillich turns for help in the clarification of the meanings of these terms.

The claim to be considered in this chapter and the next is the claim that the ambiguity of the terms 'love', 'power' and 'justice' poses an *ontological* problem. In this chapter, I shall examine certain parts of Tillich's discussion of the concepts of love and power with a view to laying bare his own conception of the problem these concepts pose. In the next chapter, I shall try to suggest why Tillich supposes that an *ontological* solution to this problem is necessary. The discussions in the two chapters will unavoidably overlap to some extent: for it is Tillich's peculiar conception of the problem about the concepts of love, power and justice which is largely responsible for his willingness to entertain the suggestion that an ontological solution to his problem is required. The emphasis in this chapter, however, will be on the sources of Tillich's interest in the meanings of the words 'love', 'power' and 'justice', while the emphasis in the

---

[3] Cf. the claim in Chapter 6 that the ontological question is generated by awareness of the 'mystery of being'.

[4] Tillich, *Love, Power and Justice*, p. 3.

The Clarification of Concepts: I

next chapter will be on Tillich's attitude towards rival conceptions of the proper approach to the solution of his problem (or problems) and on his reasons for preferring an ontological approach to its solution.

I TILLICH'S PROBLEM IN *Love, Power and Justice*

The problem tackled in *Love, Power and Justice* is said by Tillich to have two sources.[5] On the one hand, the need to investigate these concepts arises out of 'the confused state of the discussion of each of them and the even more confused discussion of their mutual relations'. On the other hand, it is traced to the 'variety of meanings in which the concepts of love, power and justice are used': these concepts, we are told, 'appear in decisive places in the doctrine of man, in psychology and sociology, they are central in ethics and jurisprudence, they determine political theory and educational method, they cannot be avoided even in mental and bodily medicine'.[6]

The first of these comments on the sources of Tillich's problem in *Love, Power and Justice* throws no light on the nature of the problem: it does not tell us why those who discuss these concepts —confusedly, it is alleged—bother to do so at all. *A fortiori*, there is no way of telling whether the philosopher, in any guise, has the right to participate in such discussions with a view to clearing up some of the 'confusions' which are said to abound in them.

The second comment—which traces Tillich's interest in these concepts to the ambiguity of the words 'love', 'power' and 'justice'—is more helpful. Even here, however, it is from the passages in the first chapter of *Love, Power and Justice* in which Tillich identifies some of the many ways in which each of these words is used, rather than from anything Tillich says about the general nature of the problem generated by the fact that these words are ambiguous, that the reader has to gather what sort of problem Tillich takes his problem to be.

[5] *Ibid.*, p. 3.
[6] *Ibid.*, p. 1.

Paul Tillich

Three strands in the problem posed by the ambiguity of the words 'love', 'power' and 'justice' should, I suggest, be distinguished. First (and most obviously), there is the problem about the actual roles played by these concepts in the various contexts in which they have an application. Secondly, there is the problem presented by the *prima facie* incompatibility of certain uses of these words with one another. The use of 'love' in the 'Great Commandment',[7] for example, is *prima facie* at odds with the use of 'love' as an emotion-word: emotions *cannot* be demanded and yet love *is* demanded in the Great Commandment. Thirdly, there is the problem held to be generated by the fact that (in the case of *each* of the words 'love', 'power' and 'justice') a *single* word is put to many dissimilar uses—the problem of rendering this fact intelligible, so that it will not have to be represented as sheerly accidental that each of these words is laden with just the ambiguity with which it is in fact laden.

About the first of these three strands in Tillich's problem, nothing need be said at this juncture, since it is clear that the clarification of ambiguous concepts is a legitimate and important task, whether or not it be represented as a distinctively philosophical one. Tillich's reason for rejecting the obvious method for the solution of the problem in this form will have to be considered in due course, however.[8]

While it will be convenient to explore the second strand by discussing a certain *prima facie* conflict between two of the uses of 'love' distinguished by Tillich, it will be found that Tillich's puzzlement in regard to these uses is also in part generated by his bafflement at the fact that a single word should have such diverse uses. Although the third strand is thus closely interwoven with the second in Tillich's discussion of the concept of love, it is also an independent determinant of his interest in the sort of conceptual problem tackled in *Love, Power and Justice*. This is most apparent in his discussion of the problem posed by the ambiguity of the word 'power': for the various uses of this

[7] 'Thou shalt *love* thy neighbour as thyself' (St Mark 12:31).
[8] See Chapter 8, Section I.

The Clarification of Concepts: I

word (unlike certain uses of the word 'love') do not even *seem* to be incompatible with one another, and yet Tillich is interested not merely in identifying and describing its various uses but also in accounting for the fact that a single word can have uses so different.

Taking for granted, then, that one of the sources of Tillich's interest in the concepts of love, power and justice is a desire to get clear about their uses in different contexts, I propose in this chapter to underscore the two other sources of his interest which have been distinguished. To this end, I shall review certain parts of his discussion of the problem posed by the ambiguity of the words 'love' and 'power'. In both cases it will be apparent that Tillich is moved to investigate these concepts by something more than curiosity about the nature of the various roles they play in different contexts—though this is, of course, *an* important source of his interest. Tillich's discussion of the concept of love serves to show how the second and third strands distinguished above are woven into the fabric of his problem, while his discussion of the meanings of the word 'power' underlines the independent importance of the third strand.

II TILLICH'S PROBLEM IN *Love, Power and Justice* AND THE *Prima Facie* INCOMPATIBILITY OF TWO USES OF THE WORD 'LOVE'

If, as is widely taken for granted, 'love' is an emotion-word designating a certain 'affection' or 'emotional state', it seems to be being misused in the commandment 'Thou shalt *love* thy neighbour as thyself'—provided it is true, as is also commonly assumed, that such emotions cannot be summoned at will. There is thus a *prima facie* conflict between the use of 'love' in the Great Commandment and its (standard?) use as an emotion-word. Since Tillich is anxious not to have to regard the Great Commandment as meaningless, he faces the problem of suggesting an interpretation of the meaning of 'love' which will *both* do justice to the use of 'love' as an emotion-word *and* make sense of the Great Commandment.

Paul Tillich

Since Tillich's escape from this difficulty is a unique one and since it sheds considerable light on the source and nature of the problem about the concept of love which he conceives it to be part of his task in *Love, Power and Justice* to grapple with, it is worth considering the solutions he rejects. No account need be taken of the 'solution' which would undercut the problem by denying the meaningfulness of the Great Commandment, since it is evident that *Tillich's* problem arises precisely because he wishes to do justice to the concept of 'love as emotion' *without* denying the meaningfulness of the Great Commandment. But consistently with granting the existence of Tillich's problem, there are (at least) two lines along which a solution might be sought. In the first place, the assumption that it is impossible for love, *qua* emotion, to be 'intentionally produced' might be rejected: and of course if it were *possible* for such an emotion as love to be deliberately summoned, the demand embodied in the Great Commandment could not be dismissed as sheerly absurd. Alternatively, an attempt might be made to make sense of the Great Commandment without denying that emotions cannot be demanded, by insisting on the ambiguity of the word 'love', by drawing attention, specifically, to the *difference* between its use as an emotion-word and its use in the Great Commandment.

The first of these solutions is dismissed quite explicitly by Tillich. His reason for holding that 'emotions cannot be demanded' is that we cannot even 'demand them of ourselves'. And in support of the claim that we cannot 'demand them of ourselves', Tillich argues that 'if we try, something artificial is produced which shows the traits of what had to be suppressed in its production'. For example, 'repentance, intentionally produced, hides self-complacency in perversion'. Again, 'love, intentionally produced, shows indifference or hostility in perversion'.[9]

There is no explicit consideration of the second solution. Tillich's rejection of it, together with his reason for considering it unsatisfactory, must be inferred from the quite different (although at first glance also quite similar) solution he himself

[9] *Love, Power and Justice*, p. 4.

The Clarification of Concepts: I

advocates. His own solution is presented as though it provided the obvious—indeed the only possible—alternative to what has been referred to above as the 'first solution'. Having concluded that 'love as an emotion cannot be commanded' (and it is this conclusion, of course, which embodies his rejection of the 'first solution'), Tillich continues: 'Either love is something other than emotion or the Great Commandment is meaningless. There must be something at the basis of love as emotion which justifies ... its ethical interpretation.' [10]

Now although the conclusion Tillich draws from the rejection of the 'first solution' is expressed in the disjunction: 'Either love is something other than emotion or the Great Commandment is meaningless', only one of these positions constitutes a viable alternative for him. For not only does he nowhere consider seriously the possibility that the Great Commandment might after all be meaningless, but the problem to which he is seeking a solution is in part generated by the assumption that it is *not* meaningless. Thus, the inference Tillich is in effect drawing from his demonstration that 'love as an emotion cannot be commanded' is that 'love is something other than emotion'.

This, it might be thought, is precisely the second of the solutions distinguished above. Is Tillich not simply noting that we just happen to have (at least) *two* concepts of love, one expressed in our use of 'love' as an emotion-word, the other expressed in the use of 'love' in the Great Commandment? On this view, the problem posed by the supposed incompatibility between these uses of 'love' simply disappears once the supposition that they are incompatible is undermined: and this supposition is effectively undermined, of course, by the mere observation that these uses are *different*.

This, however, is not quite the solution Tillich wishes to recommend. Instead of straightforwardly conceding that the word 'love' is radically ambiguous, that we have (at least) two concepts of love, Tillich wants to advance a *single* interpretation of the meaning of the word 'love' which will *simultaneously* (a)

[10] *Ibid.*, pp. 4–5.

Paul Tillich

make sense of the Great Commandment, *and* (b) do justice to those sentences in which 'love' stands for an emotion. When he concludes that 'love is something other than emotion', he does *not* seem to mean merely that there is a type of love which is not an emotion—in addition, that is, to the type of love which *is* an emotion. (This, of course, is the essence of the 'second solution'.) Nor is he claiming that 'love' is never (legitimately) used to refer to an emotion. Rather, assuming that there must be some single interpretation of the meaning of the word 'love' which will do justice simultaneously to all its diverse uses (including both its use as an emotion-word and its use in the Great Commandment), Tillich is denying the adequacy of the 'emotional interpretation', according to which love *as such* is an emotion. And this interpretation is held to be defective precisely because it does not enable us to make sense (simultaneously) *both* of the Great Commandment *and* of sentences in which 'love' refers to an emotion.

It is important to emphasise that Tillich's search for a single interpretation of the meaning of the word 'love' does not (in his own view) commit him to denying that the word 'love' is often used to designate an emotion of a certain sort. He wishes to advance a single interpretation of the meaning of the word 'love' *without* denying that there is some difference between, for example, the way in which the word 'love' is used in the Great Commandment and the way in which it is used in sentences in which it refers to a certain sort of emotion. He contrives to have it both ways without exposing his position to the charge of sheer incoherence by distinguishing between the *root-meaning* [11] of the word 'love' and its various derivative meanings. It is then possible for him to claim that his definition of 'love' (which embodies, of

---

[11] On the first page of *Love, Power and Justice* the *root-meanings* of concepts are described as 'determining their use in the different situations to which they are applied'. To search for the root-meaning of such a concept is to search for its 'basic meaning', where its basic meaning 'would precede in logical validity the variety of meanings which could be derived from it' (*Love, Power and Justice*, pp. 1–2). (For further discussion of the nature and significance of Tillich's search for the root-meanings of concepts, see Chapter 8.)

course, that single interpretation of its meaning which he demands) purports to identify the *root*-meaning merely of the word 'love', thus leaving him free with consistency to concede that the word may well have several *derivative* meanings.

But why does Tillich make the assumption that 'love' has only one (root-)meaning? The answer, I think, is that he thinks it *must* have—since only so can the fact that the single word 'love' is used in a variety of ways be rendered intelligible. Since he does not deny that the word 'love' is used in a number of different ways, his acceptance of the assumption that it must have a single meaning commits him, not to the one-word one-meaning dogma, but to the one-word one-*root*-meaning dogma. Now, although this dogma is in the short run less perverse than the one-word one-meaning dogma—since it at least does not involve any gratuitous denial of the fact that there are ambiguous words—it is perhaps in the long run more confusing. For not only does it provide a far from convincing—and a very far from inevitable—solution to the problem held to be presented by the (allegedly puzzling) fact that ambiguous words often have several, quite dissimilar, uses, but it affords Tillich a means of claiming that the way to get clear about the various meanings of an ambiguous word is to search for its *root*-meaning, *not* to examine the various ways in which it is used in the contexts in which it has an application.[12]

III TILLICH'S PROBLEM IN *Love, Power and Justice* AND THE ONE-WORD ONE-ROOT-MEANING DOGMA

A review of Tillich's account of the various meanings of the word 'power' will serve to confirm the very important role the one-word one-root-meaning dogma plays in giving rise to his problem about the concept of power. It will also serve to bring out the connection between his adherence to this dogma and his puzzlement in regard to the fact that the word 'power' has the various uses he distinguishes—a fact which he is apparently not

---

[12] See Chapter 8 for further discussion of these points.

Paul Tillich

content to attribute to the occurrence of those historical accidents which it is part of the job of etymologists to recount.

Tillich's discussion of the concept of power opens with the observation that the word 'power' is used in a number of different ways. 'Power' is what was made available at a low price by the setting up of the Tennessee Valley Authority. Again, 'the term "power" can be applied to all physical causes, although theoretical physics has got rid of this anthropomorphic symbol and has replaced it by mathematical equations. But even present-day physics speaks of power-fields in order to describe the basic structures of the material world.' Finally, 'power is a sociological category'. Thus, 'power' is used not only (in popular parlance) to refer to electric power, but it also plays a central role in 'the most abstract analysis of physical occurrences' as well as in descriptions offered by social scientists of 'the social realm'.[13]

The question generated by the fact that 'power' is used in these different ways is, according to Tillich, the question: 'How is it possible that both physics and social science use the same word, "power"?' And this is taken by Tillich to be a reasonable question because he is convinced that 'there *must* be a point of identity between the structure of the social and the structure of the physical world' and that 'this identity *must* be manifest in the common use of the term "power" '.[14]

Tillich's interest in the meaning of the word 'power' is thus aroused by the fact that the word is used in a number of different ways, when this fact is interpreted in the light of the conviction that the word *must* have a single (root-)meaning. No attempt is made to ground the problem about the meaning of the word in any felt incompatibility between its various uses.

Nor is this surprising. For there is an interesting difference between the ambiguity of the word 'love' and the ambiguity of the word 'power'. In the case of the word 'love' the claim that 'love' always really designates an emotion is sufficiently plausible

---

[13] *Love, Power and Justice*, p. 7.
[14] *Ibid.*, p. 7 (my italics).

The Clarification of Concepts: I

for it to be difficult to see what, if anything, the Great Commandment means. There is a problem about the use of 'love' in the Great Commandment precisely because there is a disposition to assert (initially at any rate) *both* that the love demanded *must* be an emotion (for is 'love' not just an emotion-word?) *and* that the love demanded *cannot* be an emotion (since emotions cannot be summoned at will). Consequently, it can plausibly be claimed that a source of puzzlement in regard to the concept of love is the apparent *conflict* between two ways in which the term 'love' is used, and not the mere fact that it happens to be used in several different ways. In the case of the word 'power', however, Tillich could not plausibly have claimed that puzzlement in regard to its meaning is generated by any *felt incompatibility* between its various uses. The fact that complicated social, political and legal manœuvres are often necessary to hold in check the 'power' of pressure-groups is not a reason for supposing that such manœuvres are necessary if 'power' is to be cut off at a generating-station. Nor do physicists who perform experiments relating to 'power-fields' suppose that their findings give them any insight into the dynamics of 'power' struggles in the social and political spheres. There is so general a recognition of the ambiguity of the word 'power' that there is *no* disposition to suppose that there is any incompatibility between the way in which the electrician uses the term 'power' and the way in which the social scientist uses it, or between the way in which the social scientist uses it and the way in which the physicist uses it.

Consequently, Tillich's claim that there is a problem about the meaning of the word 'power' seems to be based simply [15] on his conviction that the word 'power', despite its ambiguity, must have a single (basic) meaning. This conviction, in turn, seems to be grounded in his belief that the use of the single word 'power' in ways so apparently different as those he has described would be unintelligible, if, in addition to its many specialised

---

[15] It is not my intention to deny, of course, what (as was intimated in Section I) was to be taken for granted throughout this chapter—viz. that *one* of the questions in which Tillich is interested is that about the *nature* of the various meanings of the word 'power'.

Paul Tillich

meanings, it did not have a single 'root-meaning'. This, I take it, is the general import of the passage which immediately follows his enumeration of the various meanings of the word 'power': 'We must ask, how is it possible that both physics and social science use the same word "power"? There must be a point of identity between the structure of the social and the structure of the physical world. And this identity must be manifest in the common use of the term "power".'[16]

Thus, even if there were some doubt that Tillich's problem about the concept of love is in part generated by his subscription to the one-word one-root-meaning dogma, there can be no doubt that it is his subscription to this dogma which enables him to claim that the diverse uses of the word 'power' pose a philosophical problem. There can be no doubt for two reasons. In the first place, no other plausible explanation of Tillich's puzzlement [17] at the diversity of the uses of the word 'power' seems to be available. (Tillich's puzzlement in regard to the meaning of the word 'love' can, by contrast, be otherwise accounted for.[18]) Secondly, Tillich states explicitly both that the word 'power' must have a root-meaning which manifests itself in the common uses of the word and that the reason why there must be such a root-meaning is that there must be some explanation of the fact that it is 'possible that both physics and social science use the same word "power" '.[19]

---

[16] *Love, Power and Justice*, p. 7.
[17] 'Puzzlement' needs to be contrasted here with 'curiosity' to forestall the objection that Tillich's interest in the various uses of the word 'power' is to some extent independent of his subscription to the one-word one-root-meaning dogma—simply because the diverse uses of the word need to be catalogued and delineated.
[18] Cf. Section II.
[19] *Love, Power and Justice*, p. 7.

Chapter 8

THE CLARIFICATION OF CONCEPTS: II

Three strands in Tillich's problem concerning the concepts of love, power and justice have been distinguished. All three have something to do with the fact that the words 'love', 'power' and 'justice' are ambiguous. The first merely requires of the philosopher some attempt to differentiate and describe the various uses of these words. The second requires of him some comment on the *prima facie* incompatibility of certain of these uses with one another. The third requires him to illumine the allegedly puzzling fact that each of the words 'love', 'power' and 'justice' is the bearer of many different meanings. Tillich's resort, in dealing with all three phases of his problem, is to the hypothesis that the words 'love', 'power' and 'justice' have a *root-meaning*. This root-meaning is the determinant of their various specialised uses: an understanding of *it*, consequently, holds the key to the understanding of these specialised uses (and therefore also to the harmonisation of any of these uses which have the appearance of being mutually incompatible).[1] Moreover, the hypothesis that these words have a root-meaning in addition to the many meanings which make them ambiguous is just the sort of hypothesis Tillich seems to require to account for the allegedly puzzling fact that they have several different uses.[2]

Now, although Tillich's problem about the concepts of love, power and justice is regarded by him as requiring for its solution an inquiry into the 'root-meanings' of the terms 'love', 'power'

[1] Cf. Strands 1 and 2 of Tillich's problem.
[2] Cf. Strand 3 of Tillich's probem.

and 'justice', he is in fact confronted by two quite different problems: consequently no single investigation (and *a fortiori* no such investigation as he envisages) is capable of yielding solutions to both of them simultaneously. The problem of elucidating in detail the various uses of ambiguous words is a problem of quite a different sort from the problem of accounting for the fact that there are in our language words which happen to be used in a number of different ways. While the former requires for its solution the careful examination of the various ways in which ambiguous words are actually used, the latter seems to require an inquiry into the history of the uses of these words—an inquiry designed to trace the various current meanings of ambiguous words back to their source in their root-meanings.

With a view to clarifying the nature of the special (ontological) inquiry into the root-meanings of the terms 'love', 'power' and 'justice' which Tillich regards as essential to the clarification of the meanings of these terms, I propose to contrast it with the procedures he would have been committed to adopting had he distinguished between these two problems instead of regarding them as but phases or aspects of a single problem. It will be shown (1) that 'ontology', conceived as an inquiry into the root-meanings of ambiguous words, is different in certain essential respects both from 'conceptual analysis'[3] and from etymology; (2) that Tillich rejects these alternative approaches to the solution of his problems in *Love, Power and Justice* for insufficient reasons; and (3) that the procedure he recommends is a sort of hybrid of the methods he rejects.

I 'CONCEPTUAL ANALYSIS' AND THE SEARCH FOR ROOT-MEANINGS

In view of the fact that Tillich claims (when discussing the various meanings of the word 'power') that its *root-meaning*

[3] I propose to use the expression 'conceptual analysis' throughout this chapter to refer to the sort of conceptual inquiry which has as its object the clarification of the meanings of words and which seeks to achieve this end by scrutinising the ways in which such words are actually used in the contexts in which they have an application.

The Clarification of Concepts: II

must be manifest in the 'common use of the word "power" ', it might be supposed that Tillich would be committed to scrutinising the ordinary ways in which the word 'power' is used with a view to discriminating a common element within these uses. Tillich's conclusion, however, is that 'there is only one way of discovering the root-meaning of power, namely to ask about its ontological foundation'.

> 'None of the three concepts, love, power, and justice can be defined, described and understood in their varied meanings without an ontological analysis of their root-meanings. None of the confusions and ambiguities in the use of the three concepts can be removed, none of the problems intrinsic in them can be solved without an answer to the question: How are love, power and justice rooted in the nature of being as such?' [4]

Tillich's reason for rejecting what seems to be the obvious (not to say the only possible) way of clarifying the meanings of the words 'love', 'power' and 'justice' is indicated in a perplexingly brief passage on the very first page of *Love, Power and Justice*. Having argued that an examination of the concepts of love, power and justice (i.e. an inquiry into the meanings of the words 'love', 'power' and 'justice') is *necessary*,[5] Tillich insists that such a 'special inquiry' is '*almost impossible* because nobody is an expert in all the realms in which the three concepts play an outstanding role'.[6] What does Tillich mean here by 'almost impossible'? Does he mean that it is '*almost* impossible'—as distinct from 'impossible' *tout court*—because the possibility of someone being found with sufficient command of all the 'realms' in question to undertake such a conceptual investigation cannot be ruled out, however unlikely it may seem to be that there should be a person with knowledge so comprehensive and gifts so varied?

---

[4] Tillich, *Love, Power and Justice*, p. 7.
[5] It is held by Tillich to be necessary for them to be made the subject of a 'special inquiry' because 'no analysis and no synthesis in any of the spheres in which they appear can avoid referring to them in a significant and often a decisive way'.
[6] *Love, Power and Justice*, p. 1 (my italics).

Paul Tillich

This cannot be what Tillich means. His reason for saying that a 'special inquiry' into the concepts of love, power and justice is 'almost impossible' is that *nobody* is an expert in all the 'realms' in question: the availability of such an expert being categorically denied, it would be impossible for Tillich to make the possibility of a 'special inquiry' hinge upon the availability of such an expert *and still* say of this inquiry that it is '*almost* impossible', rather than 'impossible' *tout court*. For clearly, if the possibility of a 'special inquiry' *were* contingent upon the availability of the sort of expert Tillich envisages, then the assertion that there is no such expert would require him to deny *outright* the possibility of such a 'special inquiry'.

But if Tillich does not mean this sort of thing by the expression 'almost impossible', how is its force to be construed? Obscure though his manner of expressing himself is in this passage, there is no doubt, I think, that Tillich's reason for saying that a 'special inquiry' into the concepts of love, power and justice is '*almost* impossible' is simply that he holds it to be *possible* for such an inquiry to be undertaken *despite* the fact that 'nobody is an expert in all the realms in which the three concepts play an outstanding role'—*provided* the ontological character of such an inquiry is recognised. Thus, while it *would* (in Tillich's view) be impossible (*tout court*) for the meanings of the terms 'love', 'power' and 'justice' to be clarified *if* this involved examination of their actual roles in all the contexts in which they figure importantly, he holds that it is not in fact impossible for these concepts to be clarified—precisely because their clarification involves, *not* examination of their actual uses in various contexts, but a search for their *root-meanings*.

That Tillich's postulation of root-meanings for each of these terms owes something to its usefulness in facilitating the clarification of the concepts of love, power and justice is suggested by the way in which he moves from rejection of the 'conceptual analytic' approach to advocacy of the ontological approach.

'It is necessary, although almost impossible, to make them [i.e.

The Clarification of Concepts: II

these three concepts] the subject of a special inquiry. It is necessary because no analysis and no synthesis in any of the spheres in which they appear can avoid referring to them in a significant and often in a decisive way. Yet it is almost impossible because nobody is an expert in all the realms in which the three concepts play an outstanding role. *Therefore one must* ask whether there is a *root meaning* in each of these concepts, *determining their use in the different situations to which they are applied.* Such a basic meaning would precede in logical validity the variety of meanings *which could be derived from it. Therefore*, the search for the basic meaning of love, power and justice individually must be our first task ... Their elaboration is the work of ontology. Ontology is the way in which the root meaning of all principles and also of the three concepts of our subject can be found.'[7]

It is not, I think, to read something into Tillich's argument here to attribute to him the view that the ontological approach to the clarification of the concepts of love, power and justice (together with the postulation of root-meanings for these terms which adoption of such an approach requires) is in some measure justified (in his view) by the unavailability of what must seem, at first glance, to be the obvious (indeed the only) solution to his problem. For immediately after registering his conviction that 'nobody is an expert in all the realms in which the three concepts play an outstanding role' (and the availability of just such an expert is thought by him to be a necessary condition of execution of the programme of 'conceptual analysis'), Tillich writes: '*Therefore*, one *must* ask whether there is a root-meaning in each of these concepts, determining their use in the different situations to which they are applied'. What can Tillich mean by the words 'therefore' and 'must' if he does not suppose that *part* of the justification for his postulation of root-meanings for these terms (part, consequently, of his justification of an 'ontological approach' to the clarification of these concepts) lies in the impossibility of the sort of critical examination of the actual roles played

[7] *Ibid.*, pp. 1-2 (my italics).

Paul Tillich

by these concepts in various contexts which would require the existence of an 'expert in all the realms in which the three concepts play an outstanding role'? When he continues, 'Such a basic meaning would precede in logical validity the variety of meanings which could be derived from it. *Therefore*, the search for the basic meaning of love, power and justice individually must be our first task', he is surely implying that *one* thing to be said in favour of the hypothesis that there are 'root-meanings' is that a grasp of these 'root-meanings' (of the sort that 'ontological research' would allegedly make possible) would throw light on those very 'specialised meanings' of 'love', 'power' and 'justice' which he is anxious to get clear about—and about which it is said to be impossible to get clear by painstaking exploration of the actual uses of these words in various contexts.

It is easy, however, to show that *this* argument for the adoption of an 'ontological approach'—whatever the weight attached to it by Tillich—is quite unsatisfactory. For not only is the inference from the unavailability of a viable 'conceptual analytic' approach to the need for an ontological approach indefensible—both because there is no need to assume that there is *any* alternative to 'conceptual analysis' and because there would be no need to restrict the alternatives (if there were such) to the ontological programme outlined by Tillich—but (more important) his premiss is clearly false. The claim that it is impossible for there to be the sort of 'special inquiry' into these concepts which would consist in an examination of the roles they actually play in various contexts may be challenged on two grounds. (1) It is not necessary for the 'conceptual analyst' to be an 'expert' in the fields he is required to explore—if an 'expert' is one in secure possession of all the knowledge and trained in all the skills which make it possible for a specialist to make an original contribution in his special field: it may be sufficient that he be conversant with the *major* assumptions, procedures and discoveries in the fields to be investigated. Consequently, Tillich's claim that 'nobody is an expert in all the realms in which the three concepts play an outstanding role' is either irrelevant or false. It is irrelevant if

The Clarification of Concepts: II

Tillich is thinking of the sort of expert whose knowledge and training fit him to make an original contribution within his special field: for no such expertise need be possessed by the 'conceptual analyst'. It is false, however, if Tillich is thinking of the more modest sort of expertise referred to above as probably a necessary condition of 'conceptual analysis'. In either case, the crucial claim that it is impossible for there to be the sort of 'special inquiry' into these concepts which would consist in an examination of the roles they actually play in various contexts has not been substantiated. (2) Even if it should prove to be beyond the capacity of one man to achieve the sort of mastery of the various 'realms' in which 'love', 'power' and 'justice' play important roles which is necessary if 'conceptual analysis' is to be possible—and for the purpose of stating this objection it can be left undetermined just *what* sort of mastery this is—there is no reason why 'conceptual analysts' should not collaborate with one another in their investigations, complementing one another's deficiencies.

To sum up. The obvious way to clarify the concepts of love, power and justice—and this is one of Tillich's problems in *Love, Power and Justice*—is to examine the roles they actually play in the various contexts in which they have an application. Tillich turns his back quite deliberately, however, on this 'conceptual analytic' programme. I have tried to show that *part*, at least, of what induces him to do so is the curious belief that it is impossible for such a programme to be undertaken. I have also argued that the hypothesis that each of the words 'love', 'power' and 'justice' has a 'root-meaning' is one which commends itself to him, not only because justice can thereby be done to the fact that, in each case, a single word has a large number of *prima facie* different and unconnected uses,[8] but also because a means is thereby afforded him of ascertaining the various specialised meanings of these terms *without* examining their uses in the various contexts in which they have a role to play. Finally, I have argued that

[8] See Chapter 7 for a discussion of this source of the hypothesis that ambiguous words have 'root-meanings'.

Paul Tillich

the belief that a necessary condition of the possibility of 'conceptual analysis' remains unfulfilled is false: consequently, to the extent to which Tillich's advocacy of an 'ontological' programme for the clarification of the concepts of love, power and justice derives from this belief, it is without justification.

II ETYMOLOGY AND THE SEARCH FOR ROOT-MEANINGS

Just as the obvious way to clarify ambiguous concepts is to examine the roles they play in the various contexts in which they have an application, so the obvious way of throwing light on the (surprising?) fact that there are ambiguous words in our language is to trace the many meanings of these words back to their source in their root-meanings. For if it could be shown (by the etymologist) in what ways and by what stages words which once had a single meaning have acquired the many meanings they now have, then justice might be done to Tillich's feeling that it cannot be accidental that ambiguous words (like 'love', 'power' and 'justice') are laden with just the ambiguity with which they are in fact laden.

There are two things, moreover, which suggest that Tillich might be prepared to seek the assistance of the etymologist in this connection. The first is that it is by undertaking an inquiry into what he calls their 'root-meanings' that Tillich hopes to be able to diminish his own puzzlement in regard to the fact that such words as 'love', 'power' and 'justice' are the bearers of many meanings: and it is the professional responsibility of the etymologist, of course, to investigate the root-meanings of words. The second is that there is an important passage in the second volume of *Systematic Theology* in which Tillich states explicitly that 'one of the ways to determine the meaning of an abused word is the etymological one' and then goes on to describe the etymological method as consisting in going back to the 'root-meaning' of such a word in order to 'try to gain a new understanding [of it] out of its roots'.[9] What prompts his advocacy of the 'etymological

[9] Tillich, *Systematic Theology* (Vol. II), p. 21.

The Clarification of Concepts: II

method' in this passage, moreover, is just the sort of problem which is the occasion of his interest in the meaning of the words 'love', 'power' and 'justice'—the problem presented by the fact that certain words have widely varying uses in different contexts.

> 'Today whoever uses terms like "existence", "existential", or "existentialism" is obliged to show the way in which he uses them and the reasons why. He must be aware of the many ambiguities with which these words are burdened, in part avoidable, in part unavoidable.[10]
>
> 'Further, he must show to which past and present attitudes and words he applies these terms ... A theology which makes the correlation of existence and the Christ its central theme must justify its use of the word "existence" ... One of the ways to determine the meaning of an abused word is the etymological one, namely, to go back to its root meaning and try to gain a new understanding out of its roots'.[11]

This passage is of interest because, despite the similarity between the problem occasioned by the ambiguity of the words 'love', 'power' and 'justice' and the problem Tillich faces here in regard to the word 'existence', and despite his contention (in *Love, Power and Justice*) that 'none of the three concepts, love, power, and justice can be defined, described and understood in their varied meanings without an *ontological* analysis of their root meanings',[12] he here maintains that the problem about the 'root-meaning' of an ambiguous word is an *etymological* problem. Two related questions suggest themselves: (1) Can the 'search for root-meanings' to which Tillich is committed be construed—so far as this passage is concerned, at any rate—as a search for the original (i.e. the historically earliest) meanings of ambiguous words? (2) What is the relation between what Tillich calls the 'etymological' method and what he calls the 'ontological' method,

---

[10] Notice that Tillich claims here that certain ambiguities are 'unavoidable'. Light is cast on this curious claim by what Tillich says about 'the principle of semantic rationality'. See *Systematic Theology* (Vol. I), p. 61 *et seq.*

[11] *Ibid.* (Vol. II), p. 21.

[12] *Love, Power and Justice*, p. 10.

Paul Tillich

given that both are said (in different places) to be methods for the investigation of 'root-meanings'? It will be convenient to merge consideration of both of these questions in a comparison of the etymological method advocated in the passage quoted above and the ontological method recommended in *Love, Power and Justice*.

The similarities reduce, I think, to three. First, just as in *Love, Power and Justice* the need to use the ontological method is occasioned by the fact that certain words are ambiguous, so too, in the second volume of *Systematic Theology*, use of the etymological method is occasioned by the notice taken of the ambiguity of the word 'existence' and cognate expressions. Secondly, just as in *Love, Power and Justice* Tillich denies that the way to clarify the concepts of love, power and justice is to scrutinise the ways in which they are actually used in various contexts, so, in the second volume of *Systematic Theology*, Tillich defends his use of the etymological method for the clarification of the concept of existence against those 'nominalists' who 'consider words as conventional signs which mean nothing beyond the way in which they are used in a special group at a special time' [13]—thereby implying that the wrong way to try to get clear about the meaning of the word 'existence' is to note the ways in which it is actually used in different contexts. Finally, in both *Love, Power and Justice* and the second volume of *Systematic Theology*, there is a willingness to accord to the investigation of the 'root-meanings' of words a role in the clarification of ambiguous concepts.

There are also certain surface differences between the accounts given in *Love, Power and Justice* and the second volume of *Systematic Theology* respectively of the methods held to be appropriate for the investigation of the root meanings of problematic terms. For whereas in *Love, Power and Justice* Tillich maintains both that there is only one way of getting clear about the root meanings of concepts and that this is the ontological way, in the second volume of *Systematic Theology* Tillich claims

[13] *Systematic Theology* (Vol. II), p. 21.

The Clarification of Concepts: II

that 'one way' of determining the meaning of an abused word is the 'etymological one' and then goes on to *contrast* the use of this method with philosophy proper. 'Etymological inquiries indicate directions', he writes,[14] 'but they do not solve problems' —and then embarks upon a discussion of those more-than-merely-etymological problems about the concept of existence which it is a central part of the job of the philosopher proper to tackle. However, these signs that there is, in Tillich's opinion, some difference between the etymological method of investigating 'root-meanings' and the ontological method are belied both by the description Tillich gives in the second volume of his *Systematic Theology* of the etymological method and (even more clearly) by the use he makes of this method in the section on 'The Etymology of Existence'.

His description of the etymological method forms part of his attack on the method favoured by 'nominalists'.

'The nominalists of our day, like the old nominalists, consider words as conventional signs which mean nothing beyond the way in which they are used in a special group at a special time. The consequence of this attitude is that some words are invariably lost and must be replaced by others. But the nominalistic presupposition—that words are *only* conventional signs—must be rejected. Words are the results of the encounter of the human mind with reality. Therefore, they are not only signs but also symbols and cannot be replaced, as in the case of conventional signs, by other words. Hence they can be salvaged. Without this possiblity, new languages would continuously have had to be invented in the fields of religion and the humanities. One of the important tasks of theology is to regain the genuine power of classical terms by looking at the original encounter of mind and reality which created them.'[15]

There are two features of this account which deserve special

[14] *Ibid.*, p. 23.
[15] *Ibid.*, pp. 21–2.

Paul Tillich

attention. First, the claim that to go back to the root meaning of a word (in the sense in which it is the *etymologist*'s task to do this) involves 'looking at the original encounter of mind and reality' which 'created' the word—a claim which presupposes that 'words are the results of the encounter of the human mind with reality'. Secondly, the claim that the etymological method, so understood, is of more than merely historical interest, since it is the means whereby 'the genuine power of classical terms' may be 'regained', or (to change the metaphor) the means whereby such words may be 'salvaged'. These features of Tillich's account make it clear both how *different* the etymological method (as conceived by *him*) is from the etymological method as 'scientific' etymologists [16] would conceive of it and how difficult it is to distinguish between it and what Tillich calls the *ontological* method in *Love, Power and Justice*. For not only does the 'scientific' etymologist have to make no such assumption as that 'words are the results of the encounter of the human mind with reality' (where this assumption has for Tillich the negative implication that words are *not* 'conventional signs'), but he would be hard put to it to defend the empirical character of his discipline if it involved (as etymology for Tillich does) 'looking at the original encounter of mind and reality' which 'created' these terms. Again, the assumption that to get clear about the root-meaning of a word (in the sense in which this is the etymologist's job) is to gain a 'new understanding' of it—the *sort* of new understanding of it which will facilitate correct use of it—is one which Tillich's 'ontologist' (in *Love, Power and Justice*) certainly makes, but it is an assumption the 'scientific' etymologist does *not* make. After all, the sort

---

[16] I use the qualifying expression 'scientific' in 'scientific etymology' *merely* to mark the distinction between etymology proper and Tillichian etymology: it is only because 'etymology' has been used without any qualifying epithet in the course of the discussion of Tillich's account of the etymological method that it is necessary to use the qualifying expression 'scientific' to mark off etymology proper from Tillichian etymology, despite the fact that it is Tillich's conception of etymology which is unusual. In using the qualifying expression 'scientific', however, it is no part of my intention to beg any questions there may be concerning the status of etymology proper: in particular, I do not wish to imply that etymology proper is a scientific, as distinct from a historical, discipline.

The Clarification of Concepts: II

of account of the root-meaning of an ambiguous word which the 'scientific' etymologist might hope to be able to provide cannot be regarded as tantamount to an elucidation of the various current meanings of the word: to know how a word was *once* (perhaps *originally*) used is not necessarily to be any the wiser about the various ways in which it is *now* used.

The passage [17] in which Tillich puts this method to work on the clarification of the word 'existence' illustrates perfectly the gulf which separates the etymological method as *Tillich* understands it from the method employed by the 'scientific' etymologist, and, by the same token, makes it difficult to drive any wedge between it (i.e. Tillich's etymological method) and the method advocated in *Love, Power and Justice*. Taking for granted (reasonably enough) that the etymology of the word 'existence' may best be explored by tracing the *verb* 'to exist' to its origins, Tillich notes that 'to exist' derives from the Latin '*existere*', which, in turn, is the product of the verb '*stare*' (meaning 'to stand') and the preposition '*ex*' (meaning 'out of'): the verb 'to exist', then, derives from Latin words, the original meaning of which is 'to stand out of'. Thus far, Tillich's account is just what one would expect of the 'scientific' etymologist. But it is by no means the whole of the account he feels entitled to offer on the basis of his employment of what *he* calls the 'etymological' method. For having noted that the root meaning of 'to exist' is 'to stand out of', he asks: ' "To stand out of what?" ' Since ' "standing out" in the sense of "*existere*" means that existence is a common characteristic of all things', Tillich concludes that 'the general answer to the question of what we stand out of is that we stand out of non-being'. Since the Greek philosophers have taught us (according to Tillich) that 'non-being can be understood in two ways' ('namely, as *ouk on*, that is, absolute non-being, or as *me on*, that is, relative non-being') this general answer has to be specified in two ways. On the one hand, 'existing can mean standing out of absolute non-being; it can mean finitude, the unity of being and non-being'; on the

[17] *Systematic Theology* (Vol. II), pp. 22–3.

Paul Tillich

other hand, 'existing can mean standing out of relative non-being, while remaining in it; it can mean actuality, the unity of actual being and the resistance against it'. Now *all* this—and not simply that the Latin root of 'to exist' is *'existere'*—Tillich claims to have discovered in the course of his 'etymological inquiry'.[18] Yet of all this, only the claim that 'to exist' derives from the Latin *'existere'* is such that it could in principle be confirmed (or refuted) by the 'scientific' etymologist; everything else he says about the root-meaning of 'to exist' is said, presumably, on the basis of an attempt to reconstruct that 'original encounter' between the 'human mind' and 'reality' which must, on Tillich's view, have given rise to the use of *'existere'*. But if this is 'etymology' for Tillich then it is a discipline which bears little resemblance to 'scientific' etymology. Now while it is relatively easy to distinguish between 'scientific' etymology and ontology (as Tillich describes it in *Love, Power and Justice*)—to say, for example, that the former is (at least in part) an inquiry into the root-meanings of words where their root-meanings are the meanings they originally had (their earliest ascertainable meanings that is), while the latter is an attempt to ascertain the root-meanings of words where their 'root-meanings' are the meanings which underlie and are determinative of their various subsidiary meanings—it is not at all clear even *that* there is a difference between Tillichian etymology (as that is described and illustrated in the second volume of his *Systematic Theology*) and the sort of inquiry into root-meanings advocated in *Love, Power and Justice*.

Whether or not there be some (marginal) difference between etymology as Tillich conceives of it and ontology, it is quite clear that there is a marked difference between both Tillichian etymology and ontology on the one hand and 'scientific' etymology on the other. Consequently, Tillich's espousal of the etymological method of getting clear about the root-meanings of

[18] Cf. '*Summarising our etymological inquiry, we can say:* Existing can mean standing out of absolute nonbeing, while remaining in it; it can mean finitude, the unity of being and nonbeing. And existing can mean standing out of relative nonbeing, while remaining in it; it can mean actuality, the unity of actual being and the resistance against it.' (My italics.) (*Systematic Theology* (Vol. II), p. 23.)

The Clarification of Concepts: II

ambiguous words is not in conflict with his tacit rejection (in *Love, Power and Justice*) of the method of 'scientific' etymology. Since Tillich does not so much as consider the claims of this method—despite its obvious fitness to serve him in his quest for an explanation of the fact that there are ambiguous words in our language—it must be a matter of conjecture why he does not make use of it. The explanation I wish to propose is that Tillich's problem in *Love, Power and Justice* is in part a problem about the nature of the various specialised meanings of the words 'love', 'power' and 'justice', and there is no reason to suppose that *this* problem is likely to be solved by employment of the method of 'scientific' etymology: there is no reason to suppose, that is, that light is likely to be shed on the various specialised ways in which an ambiguous word is *now* used by information (supplied by the 'scientific' etymologist) about the way in which this word was *originally* used. It is the fact that the method of 'scientific' etymology is powerless to contribute to the solution of *one* of Tillich's problems in *Love, Power and Justice*, coupled with Tillich's failure to distinguish this problem from another which also perplexes him and to the solution of which this method is highly relevant—the problem of accounting for the fact that the words 'love', 'power' and 'justice' are used in a number of different ways—which must, I suggest, be held to account for his tacit rejection of this method.

III 'CONCEPTUAL ANALYSIS', ETYMOLOGY AND THE SEARCH FOR ROOT-MEANINGS

Tillich's postulation of a special method for the investigation of the root-meanings of the terms 'love', 'power' and 'justice'—a method he identifies as the 'ontological' method (for a reason to be discussed in Section IV)—is the product of a conflation of two demands. On the one hand, there is the demand—which has its source in the fact that the words 'love', 'power' and 'justice' are all ambiguous—that some account be provided of the various ways in which they are used in different contexts. On

Paul Tillich

the other hand, there is the demand—which also has its source in the fact that these words are ambiguous—that some explanation be offered of the ambiguousness of these words: this is the demand that some account be given of the various ways in which these words have acquired the many meanings they now have, so that justice may be done to the feeling that it cannot be sheerly accidental that they have so many different meanings. Now these demands are simply *different*. The first requires that some *description* be provided of the various ways in which an ambiguous word is used in different contexts: and such a description will be forthcoming only if these uses are examined. The second demand, by contrast, requires that some *explanation* be provided of the fact that a single word is used in ways so different: and for the provision of such an explanation, it is clearly neither sufficient nor even necessary that an account be given of the rules governing its uses. What is needed rather is an account of the stages in the progressive acquisition (by the word in question) of the many meanings it now has. In short, the first of these demands presents a problem of 'conceptual analysis', while the second presents an etymological problem.

The special method devised by Tillich is representable, I think, as a sort of hybrid of the two methods he rejects. For the root-meaning sought by Tillich's ontologist is, like that sought by the etymologist, capable of accounting for the fact that a single word, say 'love', is now used in a number of different ways. At the same time, however, what the ontologist discovers about the root-meanings of words is supposed to throw light on the various ways in which these words are currently used: and in this respect his discoveries are like the 'conceptual analyst's' and unlike the etymologist's. This miraculous result is put within the reach of the ontologist by means of the assumption that the root-meaning of an ambiguous word is *neither* something common to all its specialised uses *nor* its original meaning but rather its 'controlling meaning'—where its 'controlling meaning' is the *source* or *ground* or *determinant* of the many meanings it has in different contexts. Since ontology is, according to Tillich,

The Clarification of Concepts: II

the 'way'[19] in which the root-meanings of words are to be determined, it is apparently held to be possible for the ontologist, precisely by ascertaining what these root-meanings are, to solve at one stroke *both* the 'conceptual analytic' problem concerning 'love', 'power' and 'justice' *and* the etymological problem they present—without the labour either of careful examination of the current uses of these words or of painstaking exploration of the history of their uses.

IV THE SEARCH FOR ROOT-MEANINGS AND ONTOLOGY

But why, it may be asked, does Tillich suppose that an investigation of the root-meanings of the words 'love', 'power' and 'justice' (even in his highly unusual sense of 'root-meaning') is an *ontological* investigation? Might he not, alternatively, have sought to advocate his special method for the investigation of 'root-meanings' without identifying such an investigation with 'ontology'? What, after all, does the clarification of the concepts of love, power and justice—even if this be taken to necessitate scrutiny of their 'root-meanings'—have to do with the investigation of the nature of being?

When, in Chapter 2 of *Love, Power and Justice,* Tillich attempts a formulation of the ontological question, he identifies it as the question: 'What are the structures, common to everything that is, to everything that participates in being?'[20] He goes on to claim that

> 'it is decisive for our purpose in these chapters to notice that the early philosophers, when they tried to speak ... about the nature of being could not do it without using words like love, power, and justice or synonyms for them. Our triad of terms points to a trinity of structures in being itself.'[21]

Thus, Tillich's reason for supposing that an investigation of the

---
[19] Cf. *Love, Power and Justice,* p. 2.
[20] *Ibid.,* p. 19.
[21] *Ibid.,* p. 1.

Paul Tillich

root-meanings of 'love', 'power' and 'justice' must needs be an *ontological* investigation is simply that he is convinced that the concepts of love, power and justice (as these would be elucidated by a philosopher who probed their root-meanings) are indispensable to the description of the nature of being. An adequate ontology must employ these concepts in its account of the 'structures which are common to everything that is'. Consequently, no distinction can be drawn (in Tillich's opinion) between ontology and an inquiry into the root-meanings of the words 'love', 'power' and 'justice'. And that is why Tillich is able to claim that 'none of the three concepts, love, power, and justice can be defined, described and understood in their varied meanings without an *ontological* analysis of their root meanings'.[22]

V CONCLUSION

Despite the fact that his primary problem in *Love, Power and Justice* is a *conceptual* problem—that is, a problem about the meanings of the words 'love', 'power' and 'justice'—Tillich insists that it requires an *ontological* solution. The claim that we cannot get clear about the meanings of these words without undertaking an investigation of the 'structures common to everything that is' is so implausible that some explanation of Tillich's conviction that these are necessarily connected is called for. I have suggested that Tillich's 'ontologisation' of his ostensibly conceptual problem is attributable (a) partly to his rejection of the view that the way to clarify the concepts of love, power and justice is to examine the ways in which they are actually employed in various contexts,[23] (b) partly to his failure to disentangle his primary problem about the nature of the various roles these concepts play in different contexts from a different problem about these concepts—viz. the problem held to be presented by the (allegedly puzzling) fact that each of the words 'love', 'power' and 'justice' is the bearer of many meanings —and to his related failure to so much as consider the suggestion

[22] *Ibid.*, p. 10.
[23] Cf. Section I.

The Clarification of Concepts: II

that this latter problem is an etymological problem,[24] (c) partly to his conflation of the 'conceptual analytic' and the etymological questions generated by the ambiguity of the terms 'love', 'power' and 'justice',[25] and (d) partly to his assumption that there is a relation of identity between ontology (interpreted as an inquiry into the 'structures common to everything that is') and that special inquiry into the 'root-meanings' of ambiguous words which Tillich deems to be necessary because of (a), (b) and (c).[26]

[24] Cf. Section II.
[25] Cf. Section III.
[26] Cf. Section IV.

CONCLUSIONS

In the Preface to *Principia Ethica* G. E. Moore pointed out that many intractable philosophical controversies spring from a failure to notice that the disputants may be addressing themselves to different questions. In the spirit of Moore and those analytic philosophers who hold that the disentangling of questions which are liable to be confused or conflated is the least contentious of the tasks philosophers should undertake, I have tried in this book to sort out the various questions which have all masqueraded in Tillich's writings as '*the* ontological question'. They are astonishingly diverse. I have not been content, however, merely to display their diversity. I have also tried both to locate some of the intellectual pressures (and the confusions) which induce Tillich to ask these questions and to account for his remarkable failure to realise either their diversity or their dubiousness. In this respect my investigation of Tillich's writings has been more Wittgensteinian than Moorean in inspiration. In a perceptive account [1] of one of the differences between Moore and Wittgenstein, John Wisdom remarks that whereas Moore was inclined to regard paradoxical metaphysical statements merely as 'examples of the whoppers philosophers can tell', Wittgenstein (in his later period) had a special interest in exploring the sources of the problems to which paradoxical metaphysical doctrines are designed to provide solutions.

[1] 'Philosophical Perplexity', in *Philosophy and Psychoanalysis*, by John Wisdom.

Conclusions

My conclusions, however, lend only limited support to the common view that it is in 'linguistic confusions' (or, somewhat differently, in 'confusions about language') that metaphysics (or ontology) originates. There are, of course, linguistic confusions in Tillich's writings, as I have tried to bring out; but it is perhaps only the view of ontology discussed in the first chapter [2] which can be regarded as largely the product of linguistic confusions, and even in this case independent importance must be assigned to Tillich's interest in forging a close link between ontology and religion. Nor is Tillich's interest in ontological questions a simple product of confusions *about* language (about what it is for a word to have meaning, for example); for although there are such confusions they do not normally suffice to account for his interest. There is perhaps one case in which they do suffice: the view that it is the philosopher's job to determine what is 'common to everything that is' in order to throw light on the meaning of the verb 'to be' is a veritable paradigm of a conception of ontology generated by confusions about language. Of the sources of Tillich's other conceptions of ontology much more complicated, and varied, accounts must be offered.

Part of the upshot of my discussion in the second and third chapters is that the ontological enterprise can be generated by two kinds of interest in the religious quest: an interest on the one hand in the features of the human situation which make the religious quest an inevitable one for human beings, an interest on the other hand in the nature of the characteristic *object* of the religious quest. However sceptical we may have to be of Tillich's contention that the ontologist can cater to interests of both these sorts, to the first by elaborating a doctrine of man, to the second by developing a doctrine of God, potentially valuable claims about religion and the language of theology are embedded in Tillich's discussions of these matters. Consider, for example, the claim that the religious quest is fundamentally a response to the experience of 'existential anxiety'. This anxiety is held by Tillich to be an ineliminable anxiety, partly because (unlike

[2] On this view the ontological enterprise is simply identified with the religious quest.

Paul Tillich

certain kinds of 'pathological' anxiety) it does not arise out of false beliefs about oneself or the world, and partly because nothing can be done to change those features of the human situation in which it originates. If, for example, human beings have a natural desire for immortality, then, since they are mortal, they will necessarily be subject to the 'anxiety of death'. Consequently, if religion is to be seen, in part, as an attempt to cope with this sort of anxiety, it will be reasonable to regard human life as necessarily having a religious dimension. Now it is of course true that Tillich addresses himself insufficiently to the question whether 'existential anxiety' in its various forms is a universal human experience, allowing himself instead to infer an affirmative answer from the not altogether pellucid ontological doctrines of 'finitude' and 'estrangement'. Still, if the relevant empirical evidence (as distinct from the dubiously relevant 'ontology of man') supported an affirmative answer, a not implausible view of the role of religion in human life could be culled from Tillich's writings. Or take the suggestion (discussed in the third chapter) that it is the ontologist's task to contribute to a better understanding of the nature of the religious quest by elaborating a doctrine of God (or Being-itself). Even if (as Tillich is generally the first to insist) it is not within the competence of the ontologist to make any statements about God, there is obviously something to be said for the view that theological statements are to be understood in the light of the relation in which they stand to the religious quest, rather than as embodying cosmological hypotheses which, whatever their point, are devoid of any necessary relation to the religious needs of human beings. If such a view could be worked out—and it has to be admitted that there are only fragmentary indications in Tillich's writings as to how it might be worked out—it would serve to fix the position of theological language on the map of language. It would of course leave unsettled the question whether theological language so understood can ever be used to make true statements and it would, *a fortiori*, have absolutely no tendency to support Tillich's (occasionally advanced) contention that

Conclusions

it is the ontologist whose task it is to make such statements.

The three remaining ways of looking at ontology which have been considered in this book cannot be accounted for either by reference to Tillich's conviction that there is a close connection between the religious quest and the ontological question or by pointing to the linguistic confusions (and confusions about language) of which Tillich may sometimes be justly accused. I shall conclude by making some remarks about each of them.

The view that it is the philosopher's job to explore the conditions of the possibility of experience has a respectable ancestry. What Tillich has to say about it is open to grave objection, however, partly because he oscillates bewilderingly between two quite different versions of the view, partly because neither of these versions is articulated with sufficient care to expose the intellectual pressures which make such transcendental questions inescapable, and partly because it is unclear what the connection is supposed to be between the nature of *being* and the conditions of the possibility of *experience*.

Whether the fact that 'there is something and not nothing' is a mysterious fact and whether, if it is, it can legitimately serve as the starting-point for cosmological questions and arguments are both questions which have been variously answered in the history of philosophy. Tillich consistently rejects a negative answer to the first question; but his alternation between affirmative and negative answers to the second is one main source of the ontological doctrine that Being is 'the Power of Being in everything that is' and that 'everything that is' *is* only in virtue of its 'participation' in Being. So bafflingly opaque are such pronouncements—even when they have been traced to their source in Tillich's sense of the mysteriousness of the fact that there is a world at all—that it is difficult not to feel that Tillich would have been wiser to adhere more consistently to the view (of the force of which, as we have seen, he was not unaware) that the existence of the world would not be a 'mystery' if it could be explained. It is instructive to contrast Tillich's willingness to use the experience of the mystery of being as a springboard

Paul Tillich

for the plunge into dark ontological waters with Wittgenstein's cautious appraisal [3] of the nature and significance of this experience.

> 'I believe the best way of describing it is to say that when I have it I *wonder at the existence of the world*. And then I am inclined to use such phrases as "how extraordinary that the world should exist" ... [But] if I say "I wonder at the existence of the world" I am misusing language. Let me explain this: ... To say "I wonder at such and such being the case" only has sense if I can imagine it not to be the case ... But it is nonsense to say that I wonder at the existence of the world, because I cannot imagine it not existing.'

Although Wittgenstein has qualms (perhaps extravagant qualms [4]) about the very intelligibility of the language we use when we try to describe the experience of the 'mystery of being', he recognises in himself and others an urge to use such language in order to 'say something about the ultimate meaning of life', and of this urge he writes that it is a 'tendency of the human mind which I personally cannot help respecting deeply.'

The view discussed in the last two chapters (according to which the task of the philosopher is the clarification of concepts) is both, at one level, fundamentally correct and, at another level, monumentally wrong-headed. It is correct in that Tillich is quite right to insist on the importance of conceptual clarification and also right to regard this as a characteristically philosophical task. But it is also monumentally wrong-headed because Tillich

---

[3] Wittgenstein, 'Lecture on Ethics', *Philosophical Review* (1965), pp. 1–12.

[4] Wittgenstein is perhaps on stronger ground when he claims elsewhere ('Notes on Talks with Wittgenstein', *Philosophical Review* (1965), pp. 12–13) that our 'astonishment that anything exists ... cannot be expressed in the form of a question and there is no answer to it.' It is one thing—and perhaps implausible—to maintain that we cannot intelligibly give expression to our astonishment at the existence of the world (by using, for example, just the language Wittgenstein found it natural to use in his 'Lecture on Ethics'); it is another thing—and decidedly plausible—to hold that we cannot intelligibly set about looking for an answer to the question *why* anything exists. As Tillich himself realises at times, this question is suspect not because any answer it might fetch would be sheerly speculative but because any Being (or God) invoked in any would-be answer would be subject to the very same question.

Conclusions

allows his fixed hostility to what he calls 'nominalism' [5] and his flirtation with the delusive charms of etymology to induce him to propose ontological solutions to merely conceptual problems.

It is ironical that what Tillich seems to have regarded as his most important contribution to philosophical theology should turn out to be its gravest defect. For the ontological language in which he consciously formulates his basic doctrines is not only inessential but also presents a formidable obstacle to the very comprehension of what he has to say. So far as 'de-ontologisation' of these doctrines is a possibility, it is the course which must be followed by the sympathetic interpreter of Tillich if the undoubted insights scattered throughout his writings are to be rescued. Many of the illuminating analyses to be found in *The Courage To Be*, for example, can be salvaged, I think, in spite of the mangling they receive in the ontological mill through which they are made to pass. But there are limits to such a programme of 'de-ontologisation', partly because it is not clear in places just which ontological game is being played and partly because some of these games are not worth playing even with modified rules. Unfortunately, these limits fall far short of the point at which it would be possible to construct a characteristically Tillichian but radically 'de-ontologised' system of philosophical theology. As Tillich himself believed, the ontological cast of his system is not incidental to the system: to object to its ontological cast is to object to the system.

[5] 'The nominalists of our day, like the old nominalists, consider words as conventional signs which mean nothing beyond the way in which they are used in a special group at a special time.' *Systematic Theology* (Vol. II), pp. 21–2.

BIBLIOGRAPHY

Only works cited in the text are listed.
Tillich's works are listed in the order in which they originally appeared, though several of the editions referred to are not the original editions.

Austin, J. L., 'The Meaning of a Word', in *Philosophy and Ordinary Language* (ed. C. A. Caton) (Urbana: University of Illinois Press, 1963 (Illini Books)).

Baier, K., 'Existence', *Proceedings of the Aristotelian Society*, Vol. LXI, 1960–1.

Kegley, Charles W. and Bretall, Robert W. (eds.), *The Theology of Paul Tillich* (New York: The Macmillan Company, 1961 (Macmillan Paperback)).

Martin, Bernard, *The Existentialist Theology of Paul Tillich* (New York: Bookman Associates, 1963).

Moore, G. E., *Principia Ethica* (London: Cambridge University Press, 1903).

Tillich, Paul, *The Protestant Era* (Phoenix Books: University of Chicago Press, 1957).

—, *Systematic Theology*, Vol. 1 (London: Nisbet, 1953).

—, *The Courage To Be* (New Haven: Yale University Press, 1952).

—, *Love, Power and Justice* (New York and London: Oxford University Press, 1954).

—, *Biblical Religion and the Search for Ultimate Reality* (London: Nisbet, 1956).

Bibliography

—, 'The Relation of Metaphysics and Theology', *Review of Metaphysics* (1956) x, 57–63.
—, *Systematic Theology*, Vol. II (London: Nisbet, 1957).
—, *Theology of Culture* (New York: Oxford University Press, 1959).
—, *Systematic Theology*, Vol. III (Chicago: University of Chicago Press, 1963).
Wisdom, John, *Philosophy and Psychoanalysis* (Oxford: Basil Blackwell, 1953).
Wittgenstein, Ludwig, *Tractatus Logico-Philosophicus* (trans. D. F. Pears and B. F. McGuinness) (London: Routledge and Kegan Paul, 1961).
—, 'Lecture on Ethics', *Philosophical Review* (1965), pp. 1–12.
—, 'Notes on Talks with Wittgenstein', *Philosophical Review* (1965), pp. 12–13.

For Product Safety Concerns and Information please contact our EU
representative GPSR@taylorandfrancis.com
Taylor & Francis Verlag GmbH, Kaufingerstraße 24, 80331 München, Germany

www.ingramcontent.com/pod-product-compliance
Lightning Source LLC
Chambersburg PA
CBHW052129300426
44116CB00010B/1827